THE ROSE GARDEN
OF PERSIA

THE ROSE GARDEN OF PERSIA

BY
LOUISA STUART COSTELLO

Fredonia Books
Amsterdam, The Netherlands

The Rose Garden of Persia

by
Louisa Stuart Costello

ISBN: 1-4101-0095-2

Copyright © 2002 by Fredonia Books

Reprinted from the 1911 edition

Fredonia Books
Amsterdam, The Netherlands
http://www.fredoniabooks.com

All rights reserved, including the right to reproduce this book, or portions thereof, in any form.

In order to make original editions of historical works available to scholars at an economical price, this facsimile of the original edition of 1911 is reproduced from the best available copy and has been digitally enhanced to improve legibility, but the text remains unaltered to retain historical authenticity.

THE ROSE GARDEN
OF PERSIA

CONTENTS

	PAGE
OF PERSIAN POETRY	1
INTRODUCTION	23
ORNAMENTAL COMPOSITION	39
THE SUFIS	44
Their Tenets	45
The Object of their Devotion	47
Their Sentiments in Verse, by Hafiz	48
Ode, expressive of their Devotional Fervour	51
Favourite Subjects of Eastern Poets	54
The Most Distinguished Poets	56
FERDUSI	57
The Shah Namah	59
Satire on King Mahmoud	64
Anecdote of Sebectighin	67
Anecdote of Prince Mahmoud and his Father	69

Contents

	PAGE
Alleged Origin of the Shah Namah	71
Death of Ferdusi	74
The Gardens of the Daughters of Afrasiab. (From the Shah Namah.)	76
Heroes of Ferdusi's Poem	79
Jamshid's Courtship	81
Legend of the Simorgh, or Anca	87
Poets before Ferdusi	90
The Regrets of Bokhara. By Roduki	91

ESSEDI OF TÛS 93
   His Poem of Day and Night . . 95

UNSURI 100
   His First Meeting with Ferdusi . . 100

TOGRAY 103
   His Eulogy on Kashmeer . . . 104

MOASI, KING OF POETS . . . 108
   His Readiness at Extemporising . 109
   His Mystical Odes 110

KHAKANI 114
   His Delight in Solitude . . . 114
   His Adventure with his Patron . . 114
   His Gazel, or Amatory Poem . . 115

OMAR KHIAM, THE VOLTAIRE OF PERSIA 117
   His Profession of Faith, in Verse . 119
   His Poems 121
   His Ridicule of Predestination . . 124

Contents

	PAGE
Azz' Eddin Elmocadessi	129
His Poem on Flowers and Birds	129
Nizami	135
His Principal Works	135
The Loves of Khosrû and Shireen	135
Legend concerning Ferhâd	137
Sadi	146
His Opinion of Women	147
The Bostan and Gulistan	149
Attar	154
The Way to Paradise, from Perid Namah	154
The Moolah of Rûm	158
His Ode, The Fairest Land	160
Hafiz, the Persian Anacreon	162
Curious Dispute at his Death	163
His Tomb visited by Pilgrims	164
The Kasidah and Gazel	165
The Women of Shirâz	173
The Green Old Man	178
Jami	180
Poem of Yussuf and Zuleika	182
Profusion at Eastern Marriages	194
Beauty of Yussuf	195

Contents

	PAGE
HATIFI	204
Poem of Mejnoun and Leila	205
SCHEIK FEIZI	215
His Life	216
The Mahabarit	218
Story of Khaja Aiass and Mehr-el-Nissar	218
Poem of the Desert-Born	226

xii

OF PERSIAN POETRY

How has it come about that of all the poetries of the East, that of Persia alone has to some extent made itself at home on English soil? While Kalidasa and Hariri are practically unknown, Hafiz and Firdausi, and above all, Omar Kháyyám, have become in a measure household words among lovers of poetry in England. Yet Kalidasa's dramas are the only ones worthy of consideration outside the charmed circle which has been influenced, directly or indirectly, by the Greek drama; while Hariri holds a position in Arabic poetry which is unique in the history of Oriental literature. Yet

Of Persian Poetry

nothing is known of Kalidasa or Hariri by even well-read Englishmen, who are familiar with the adventures of Sohrab and Rustum, and regard Omar's quatrains as a sort of revelation. In poetry, Persia—and Persia alone—represents for us the East. How is this?

At first sight it might seem a mere chance result that Firdausi and Omar have been fortunate enough to find translators through whom they could make an adequate appeal to English readers. Matthew Arnold's versions from Firdausi (which, by the way, were not directly from the Persian text, but from Mohl's French prose translation) come nearest to the nobleness and simplicity of Homer in all English verse, but that nobleness and simplicity exist in a large measure in his original, and in cherishing Sohrab and Rustum we are doing homage to one of the greatest of the world's poets. And Omar? What can we say of Omar that has not been said better already by some of his innumerable worshippers?—for Omar just now is a cult, and seems to be the only religion of

Of Persian Poetry

many. How far he owes that position to FitzGerald we may discuss later, but it may be remarked here that there is no Calderon cult or Æschylus cult analogous to that of Omar, and yet FitzGerald translated both Calderon and Æschylus. We may surely, then, credit Omar with much of the qualities which have made his *Rubáiyát* the favourite of so many poets and thinkers. So our original puzzle remains: Why should these two Persian poets be the only ones that have acclimatised themselves in England?

Can we see here some subtle sympathy between the Persian Aryans and their European cousins? Professor Max Müller would probably assent to this explanation, but the high-caste Hindu has also the Aryan cousinship, and yet neither the *Ramayana* nor the *Mahabharata* has become a household word in England, and, as I have said before, Kalidasa is equally unknown here. And even as applied to Persia, the Aryan theory scarcely holds good, for there have been three periods of literary activity

Of Persian Poetry

in Persia, corresponding to three different forms of the language known to the pundits as Zend, Pahlavi, and Persian. If it were merely a question of racial sympathy, the Zendavesta or the obscure products of the Pahlavi literature should have equal claim to appeal to us as Firdausi or Omar; but it is only when the Pahlavi, or Middle Persian, becomes transformed by its contact with Arabic into Persian properly so called, that poetry written in it seems capable of appealing to the European mind.

Here, then, we seem on the threshold of an explanation of the appeal of Persian poetry to Englishmen. It is when Persia comes in contact with Islam — in other words, an Aryan race with a Semitic religion—that we see produced a tone of mind analogous and sympathetic to the European, which may also be described as Aryan tinged with Semitic religion. The analogy may even go further: just as Europe, when it took up the religion of Judæa, gave it a specific form and tone, so the Persians, when they adopted Islam, gave it a special

Of Persian Poetry

form which constitutes the sole break in the monotony of the Mohammedan religion from Timbuctoo to China. The Shiite heresy is peculiar to Persia, and has given rise (as readers of Matthew Arnold will remember) to a special religious rite represented in a Passion Play, which again has its analogies among the Semitised Aryans of Europe. Altogether, therefore, a good case may be made out for attributing the undoubted sympathy which exists between Persian poetry and the West to the remarkable analogies which exist between their spiritual lives.

Yet for poetry we need poets, and no amount of spiritual conflict between race and religion will produce poetry or poets, unless other conditions are present. It is not for three hundred years after Persia had adopted Islam that we get Persian poetry worthy of the name—I leave Rúdagí out of the account—so that the mere adoption of an alien creed was clearly not the determining cause of Persian supremacy in poetry. It was a revival of the old Persian valour,

Of Persian Poetry

and the conquering instincts which can be traced through Chosroes to Cyrus, that brought the national mind to flower in poetry, and it was at the conquering court of Mahmúd of Ghazna that Persian poetry ceased to be local, and took upon itself a world-tone. Mahmúd is said to have assembled about him a Round Table of no less than four hundred accredited poets, of whom FIRDAUSI was the king. Every one knows the story of the tragedy connected with Firdausi's great work, the *Shahnamah*, or Book of Shahs. Heine has told in German, Mr. Gosse in English, how the poet was promised a *toman* for every verse of his great work, and was then paid in silver tomans, not in gold; how in revenge he handed the sixty thousand silver tomans to the bath attendants as a *pourboire*, and then went forth into exile, from which he issued scathing satires on the Shah's somewhat beclouded ancestry; how the Shah repented him, and sent the due sixty thousand golden tomans, which reached Firdausi only when he was being carried on

Of Persian Poetry

his bier to his last resting-place. The noble scorn of the poet was a fit reflex in his own life of the tone of his great work.

Here in the *Shahnamah*, Firdausi (the Man of Paradise) had work to do analogous to that which European poets were just beginning to attempt about the same time as his epoch (940–1020). The *Song of Roland* recalls to the memory of Frenchmen one of the great heroes of their past with the same directness and nobility with which Firdausi recalls to the Persians the whole story of their past in its most heroic aspects. The *Shahnamah* resembles more, perhaps, a Malory in verse, or rather, if the many verse originals out of which Malory composed his prose romance could be brought together in one volume, and re-written by a great poet, that would resemble the *Shahnamah* of Firdausi. Curiously enough, the central incident of the whole epic—the single combat of the two heroes, father and son, in which the son falls—is reproduced almost exactly in the early heroic literature of Ireland, and suggestions have been made that there was an original Aryan myth or legend from which both these Aryan nations took the episode. This is, however, going too far; in a fighting age the natural pathos of such a situation could easily occur independently to two poetic minds. But in the fierce joy of fight, in the chivalrous character of his knights, in the nobility of his tone, Firdausi stands by the side of the best mediæval romancers.

If in the matter of his epic Firdausi is Western and mediæval, in form (like all the Persian poets) he derives from the Arabs. It is a doubtful point whether rhyme in general does not come from the practice of the Arabic poets. There is still much to be said for its derivation from Arabic Spain through Provence to all West Europe; but be this as it may, there is no doubt that the *Matherawi* used by the Persians for epic and didactic purposes comes directly from imitation of the Arabic poets. Whether there was anything in the tone of the early Arabic poems of chivalry, written in or inspired by

Of Persian Poetry

the Times of Ignorance, which influenced Persian poetry is a more obscure question. Imru'lkais is as chivalrous as any hero of Firdausi or Malory, but his exploits are not told in epic form; his were songs of triumph, written by the hero-poet himself. The matter of Firdausi's great poem comes from Persian tradition, even if the verse is couched in Arabic form, and the tone has its analogues in Arabic poems of chivalry, like those enshrined in the *Kitab Alaghani*. Before parting from Firdausi, it may be interesting to mention that his influence had lasted on down to the present century, to such an extent that there is record of an epic poem, written by a Persian in India, in honour of the great and noble George the Fourth, and entitled *Georgenamah*.

The next great name in Persian poetry is that which, by the genius of FitzGerald, has become representative of it. The main questions of the art of OMAR KHÁYYÁM (1050–1124) have been threshed out almost *ad nauseam* in these latter days. That FitzGerald represented the spirit of the *Rubáiyát*, rather than their actual contents, turns out to be somewhat of an exaggeration. Though by no means a "crib," at least the majority of his quatrains occur somewhere or other in the Persian text. FitzGerald adopted the only possible method for a translation which is to be itself literature, *i.e.* he re-wrote in the spirit of his original. The recipe is a simple one, but unless you are a poet yourself, your re-writing will scarcely be poetry. The point to notice about FitzGerald's version is, that only when he attempts to re-clothe the spirit of Omar Kháyyám does his version reach high poetic merit. He was translating all his life, from Greek, from Spanish, and he even attempted another version from the Persian, but none of these translations—meritorious as they are—are real contributions to English literature. The moral of that is surely that it is the spirit of Omar that gives value to FitzGerald, not FitzGerald that has unduly aroused admiration for Omar's merits.

Yet the universal cult of Omar cannot be altogether explained by the merit of the

Of Persian Poetry

version by which he has made his appeal. He represents a mood which is rare indeed, but occurs at intervals to almost all races. *Ecclesiastes* represents it in the Scriptures, Renan in modern French literature, Ibsen, perhaps, in the drama of the day. Disillusionment, pessimism, agnosticism—whatever we call it—comes to most men in their own lives, and to most nations at periods of transition. It were idle to guess what were the circumstances in Omar's life and surroundings that led to the quasi-agnostic pessimism and Epicureanism that have proved so attractive to the last generation of Englishmen. For there are signs that the mood which he represents is dying away. Those who care for Kipling are not likely to be enthusiastic for Omar, and the rising tide is now with the song of action.

It is possible that Omar became disillusionised by seeing the fate of his former schoolmates. One, his patron, was raised to the giddy height of a vizier, and then dashed down again: the other, the notorious Old Man of the Mountain, who founded

Of Persian Poetry

the sect of the Assassins, died in old age without suffering any punishment. Or possibly the pressure of the Turk upon his native country led him to look upon all things dismally; or perhaps he is an early example of the Faust disillusionment, when a man like Omar acquires all the knowledge of his age, and then finds that that too is vanity. By the favour of his former schoolmate, the vizier, he became astronomer-royal of Persia, and works of his are still extant on algebra and geometry, while others on astronomy and philosophy have been lost. It is clear that he had acquired all that passed for knowledge in his age, and yet he felt that the passing hour was the only reality.

It is scarcely likely that Omar's pessimism was the result of an elaborate philosophical scheme of the universe akin to that of Schopenhauer or Hartmann. Mr. John Payne, his latest translator, attempts to make out, indeed, that at the root of Omar's quatrains is an elaborate system of philosophy, akin to, if not actually derived from, the pessimistic pantheism of the Vedas. He

Of Persian Poetry

is obliged to own, indeed, that there is no evidence of the Vedas as a system being adopted or known in Persia in Omar's time, and the resemblance he notes between isolated quatrains of Omar and occasional utterances of the Vedas on the nullity of the world are scarcely more than coincidences of mood, rather than of thought. It is because Omar's philosophy is temperamental rather than didactic that it has had such an appeal in these latter days. FitzGerald has helped to give a misleading effect to Omar's poetry by his selection, and the method by which he has strung them together. In the original they are, for the most part, disjointed utterances, written, it is true, in a uniform mood of revolt and pessimism, but scarcely connected from one quatrain to another. It must be remembered that the quatrain, or *Rubáiy*, is a form of verse derived by the Persians from the Arabs, and by no means confined to Omar. Hafiz himself has nearly seventy *Rubáiyát* included in his complete works, and Sadi also wrote many *Rubáiyát*. Now, it is the essence of this form that it is

Of Persian Poetry

complete in four lines, as contrasted with the *Kasida*, which is longer and more connected, and the "Girdle Rhyme," which often extends to a considerable number of verses, all connected by a "girdle" of a single rhyme. Merely, therefore, as a consequence of the form chosen by Omar, it were idle to seek for a connected system out of his *Rubáiyát* except that connection which comes from uniformity of mood.

On the other hand, there is no reason to doubt the sincerity of the scepticism and Epicureanism displayed in Omar's verses. El Kifti, the Arab literary historian, expressly declares that his orthodoxy was doubted, and that he adopted the conventional rites, including the pilgrimage to Mecca, for prudential reasons. But for the protection of his friend the vizier, there is little doubt that Omar might have suffered severely for his bold utterances. It would be indeed strange if a set of sham sentiments should have so strong an appeal eight centuries later to men speaking a foreign tongue.

Of Persian Poetry

The attempt has been made to represent Omar's outspoken praise of the pleasures of the senses as mystical, Sufic utterances. This is but a weak invention of the enemy, and it were idle to see in the praises of wine the laudations of the mystic communion of the individual with the World Soul. That may be true of Hafiz, as we shall see, but all tradition, and the very nature of the *Rubáiyát*, indicate that Omar meant what he said in praising the *joie de vivre*. There comes a time in the life of most men devoted to study and thought when they cry out with Renan that perhaps *les gais* are right, and Omar represents that mood. He does not penetrate to the deeper stage of the Hebrew sage, with whom all is vanity— even wine and women.

True Sufic mysticism is represented by the three poets known to us by their *takhallus*, or pen-names, as Sadi, Rumi, and Hafiz. In all three we have distinct evidence of the theological Pantheism underlying their poetic utterances. SADI (1184–1292), during his wanderings in

Of Persian Poetry

India, risked his life in destroying a statue of Siva, when he detected the imposture by which the goddess was made to raise her hands in front of her worshippers; and besides this, on his return to his native place Shiraz, where he ultimately died, he preached and wrote on theology, giving in express terms his Sufic doctrines. Both his *Bustán* (Fruit Garden) and *Gulistán* (Rose Garden), the former in verse, the latter in prose intermingled with verse, give in imaginative form the same doctrine expressed in his theological works. He wrote in Hindustani and Arabic, as well as Persian, and from his Indian travels we may perhaps attribute to him what Mr. Payne without evidence attributes to Omar, some evidence of the Hindu Pantheism in his thought. RUMI (1207–1273), who took his name from dwelling in the empire of Rum or Asia Minor, showed his theological convictions by founding the order of Mawlawi Dervishes, who still exist and flourish throughout the realms of Islam. His *Mathnawái* does not, however, profess that

Of Persian Poetry

mystical identity of the body and the World Soul which is the dangerous tendency of all mysticism.

With HAFIZ (*obiit* 1391) the case is somewhat different. Many of his verses speak in all too glowing terms of the pleasures of the flesh, and it would be almost as difficult in his case to interpret these passages mystically as in the case of Omar. But it does not follow that his other verses, which deal with as much fervour with the prospects of union with the World Soul, are not equally earnest and real. Your reformed rake often makes the best of penitents, and we have the recent case of Verlaine to prove that a man may write most spiritually and most carnally. When Hafiz writes—

"The dust of this body of mine is the Veil face of the soul,
  Behind the Veil they treat me as men treat parrots,"[1]

---

[1] That is, they put the looking-glass of the world in front of man, just as those who train a

Of Persian Poetry

he is as sincere as ever Omar can be; or when at the end of one of his *Kasidas* he gives utterance to the prayer—

"Oh, come and sweep away the very existence of Hafiz,
That in Thy presence none may hear that I exist at all"—

we have the very voice of the "wearers of wool" (*Súf*), or of the followers of σοφία (whichever be the true etymology of "Sufi"). It is besides reported of him that when he heard that Mansur of Hallaj had been put to death for saying "*Ana'l hakk*" (I am the Truth),—the very central doctrine of Sufism —all that Hafiz remarked was, "He should not have divulged the mystery."

There is thus no reason to doubt the genuineness both of Hafiz's mysticism and his sybaritism. The conjunction is not so rare that it need surprise us. The very form which he chose as his favourite verse—the

parrot put a looking-glass in front of him, in order that he should think the sounds he hears come from another parrot.

Of Persian Poetry

Ghazal—lends itself to both tendencies. A number of couplets, each rhyming in the last hemistich, and the last giving the poet's name, as in the example above, can only deal with personal feelings, which for a poet are almost invariably connected with love of woman or of God. That in some way the Sufis identified the two is part of the system which renders the whole movement so interesting, and to some extent so *bizarre*. Whether we are to see any Indian influence in the whole movement, or whether it was the natural reaction against an asceticism forced upon an Aryan race by an alien creed, it would be difficult to decide. But with regard to the former supposition, it is noteworthy that the doctrine is called *Tarikat* (the Path), which certainly recalls the Four Paths of Buddhism, while the stages of perfection are each termed *Manzilhá* (roadside inn), which carries out the same conception. But by the time of Hafiz, Sufism had formed almost a convention of Persian poetry, and it is remarkable that the Sunnite or orthodox censors removed from his verse all

Of Persian Poetry

indications of his Shiite heresy, but were content to let the Sufism alone.

This conventional character of Sufism in Persian poetry is displayed in its last representative, JAMI (1414–1492). Among his numerous works (said to have amounted to ninety-nine volumes), his treatment of two of the most popular subjects of Islamic legend, *Yúsuf and Zulaikha*, and *Sálámán and Absál*, deals with the subject mystically from the Sufic standpoint. The latter has been translated by FitzGerald, and we can learn from his translation how little effective Sufic mysticism is as compared with Omar's scepticism. Yet both may be equally traced to the contrast of race and creed on which I have insisted throughout. With some—and those the rarer spirits—such a contrast leads to scepticism and doubt, and to clutching at the pleasures of the passing day; while other minds—less earnest with themselves, perhaps, but desirous of joining in the common creed —find the solution in mystic communion. Both tendencies are strong with us in England to-day. On the one hand we have the cult

Of Persian Poetry

of Omar and the agnostic creed, on the other hand Theosophy and the Society for Psychical Research. Both tendencies are represented, as we have seen, to the fullest extent in Persian poetry, and it is for this reason that these "Orient pearls at random strung," alone of all the verse of the East, have made their appeal to modern men.

JOSEPH JACOBS.

INTRODUCTION

THE softest and the richest language in the world is the Persian: it is so peculiarly adapted to the purposes of poetry, that it is acknowledged there have been more poets produced in Persia than in all the nations of Europe together: yet, except Sadi and Hafiz, and, it may be, Ferdusi,[1] there are few whose names even are known to the general English reader; and the too common impression is, that there exists a great monotony in their verse, both as to sound and sense.

This is so far from being the case, that there is perhaps in no poetry so much variety, both in style and subject, as in the

[1] To these, thanks to the popularity of Fitz-Gerald's translation, must be added the name of Omar Khiam.

musical and expressive Persian. Sir William Jones, that great authority and competent judge not only in Oriental beauties of language but in all matters of taste, has justly pronounced, that the verse of the East is "rich in forcible expressions, in bold metaphors, in sentiments full of fire, and in descriptions animated with the most lively colouring."

This secret treasure has, however, seldom been sought, except by the learned; and the idea that it belonged exclusively to that class has deterred many from endeavouring to understand it, and from availing themselves of the labours of those English, French, and German scholars who have devoted their powerful energies to render the charming but neglected study known. Still it must be confessed that it would require some perseverance, and considerable fatigue, to the admirer of Eastern literature, to seek amongst the authors in each of these languages for the precious poetical gems, which are so scattered, and so hard to find. As these difficulties did not deter me, I have been

Introduction

enabled to bring together a collection of all that pleased me most, and am in hopes that the English reader will be gratified to meet at once, without trouble, with many of the treasures he has so long slighted.

Sir William Jones remarks, in his "Preface" to a few translations: "If the novelty of the following poems should recommend them to the favour of the reader, it may, probably, be agreeable to him to know that there are many others of equal or superior merit which have never appeared in any language of Europe; and I am persuaded that a writer acquainted with the originals might imitate them very happily in his native tongue, and that the public would not be displeased to see the genuine compositions of Arabia and Persia in an English dress."

Since the period when the accomplished Orientalist wrote this, many translations in French, German, and English have appeared, but most frequently in prose; so that the ground may be considered untrodden by all but learned feet, and still as mysterious as the fabled gardens of Irem to the general reader. The beautiful specimens given to the world, from time to time, by Mr. Forbes Falconer, in *The Asiatic Journal*, are almost alone, and appear but too rarely.

The late lamented Sir Gore Ouseley, at the time of his death, was preparing a work for the press on Persian literature, which the Asiatic Society is now printing. I have been allowed, by the courtesy of that Society, to whom I am deeply indebted, to see the MS., and had I done so previously to this work being ready for publication, I should have felt my own attempt unnecessary: the accomplished author has not, however, given lyrical specimens of the poets in English.

"The mine of Persian literature," observes an elegant writer, "contains every substance, from the dazzling diamond to the useful granite, and its materials may be employed with equal success to build castles in the air or upon earth."

Poetry has ever been, and is still, held in the greatest veneration in the East, and its admirers include almost the whole popula-

Introduction

tion; respect and esteem attend on the aspirant for poetic fame, and even the smallest spark of genius is hailed with delight. The power and effect of the art are so much appreciated by the Arabs, that they have given it the name of "legitimate magic"; and "to string pearls" expresses, in their figurative language, to compose verses.

Many Eastern anecdotes are related of the early dawn of poetry in the youthful mind, and the admiration its appearance excited; amongst others, the following is characteristic: The celebrated Abderrahmân, son of Hissân, having, when a child, been stung by a wasp, the insect being one he did not recognise, he ran to his father, crying out that "he had been wounded by a creature spotted with yellow and white, like the border of his vest." On hearing these words uttered in a measure of Arabian verse, as elegant as natural, Hissan became aware of his son's genius for poetry.

The first rhythmical composition in the Persian language is recorded to have been the production of Bihrâm Goar, a prince who lived in the fifth century A.D. The occasion of his becoming a poet was this: He was tenderly attached to a female slave, named Dilârâm, who generally attended him in all his parties of pleasure. One day the prince encountered a lion when in the company of his favourite, seized him, after a struggle, *by the ears*, and, holding him captive in this manner for some time, in spite of the animal's efforts to free himself, exultingly exclaimed, in sounding verse, "I am as the raging elephant, I am as an active and mighty lion!" Dilârâm, being accustomed to reply to whatever the king said in the same strain as her royal lover, addressed him *extempore* with a fine compliment, in which, punning on his name and that of his father, she compared him to a "lofty mountain."

Bihrâm, being struck with the cadence and jingle of these accidental verses, pointed out their beauties to the learned men of his court, and desired them to produce something in imitation. This they accordingly

Introduction

attempted, but without ever exceeding a single distich in any of their compositions.

Several other origins are given by the Persians to their earliest poetry, but, except occasional lines more beautiful to the ear than the mind, there is little known before the tenth century of the Christian era.

The first poem, expressing sentiment, to be met with in Persian records, is the following:—

"Why should the antelope, as once of yore,
Bound o'er the plain, as swiftly as before?
Alas! why should his boasted speed be tried,
To quit the spot where those he loves abide?"

Bigotry and ignorance combined to prevent the growth of poetry in Persia, as well as in most other countries. It is related of one of their princes that on a manuscript being shown him, containing a poetical history of the loves of Wâmik and Asrah, he exclaimed that the Koran was the only book he desired his subjects to read, and commanded it to be burned, together with any others found in his dominions. Arabic continued long to be the court language, used in all transactions of state, the native Persian being thought barbarous and impolite, in the same manner as in early times the French superseded the native English in our own country. Ferdusi was the Chaucer of Persia, but there were a few others, as with us, who had already struggled to break the way for the great poet.

In poetical composition there is much art used by Eastern writers, and the arrangement of their language is a work of great care. Numerous are the rules by which they must guide themselves in their verses; as, for instance, the *art*, which in Arabic signifies *setting jewels*, by which words are selected which bear a similarity in sound. Of this custom, varied in a number of ways, and all considered to possess great merit in a skilful hand, we have, in the poetry of the troubadours and early French and English writers, many examples. In translation this would appear little better than a string of puns.

One favourite measure is called Sujá, literally *the cooing of doves*, and it frequently

Introduction

ends a poem. The *letters* must be equal or the same, and the rhyme agreeing: the same *word* must sometimes appear in different parts of the distich; sometimes an anagram must be made; sometimes the sentence must be capable of being read backwards and forwards. To attempt examples of these punning conceits would be useless and little desirable; of course, in the original language alone could they be understood. The following is one of the easiest:—

> "They call me *madman*—if 'tis so,
> Bind with thy locks that softly flow
> The *madman*, that at least he be
> Held in thy chains and slave to thee."

The poetical compositions of the Persians are of several kinds. The Gazel, or Ode, literally signifies taking delight in the society of the fair sex, and is used technically for several couplets composed in one measure. As a general rule, the Gazel should not contain more than twelve distichs, though some poets have greatly exceeded this length. The usual subjects of the Gazels are beauty, love, or friendship; but frequently they are employed to set forth the praises of wine, and many treat of the mysteries of the Sufis. The poet generally introduces his name in the last couplet.

The Kassideh, or Idyl, resembles the Gazel, except that it has more distichs. It may consist of either praise or satire, morality or other subjects. The Persians do not extend the length beyond one hundred and twenty distichs; but the Arabians sometimes make it exceed five hundred.

The Tushbib signifies a representation of the season of youth and beauty, descriptions of love, praise, or a relation of circumstances.

The Mesnavi is called *wedded*, its rhymes and measure being even, and each distich having distinct endings.

The other measures are less common, or, at least, their explanation is less required, as their peculiarities could scarcely be made sensible to the reader of an English translation.

"When Niebuhr and his scientific companions," remarks a writer on Eastern literature, "set out on their travels to the East,

Introduction

they were instructed by their patron, the King of Denmark, to have *nothing to do with poetry*. But he might as well have shut the book of knowledge from them at once; for the fact is, that in the Arabic, as well as Persian language, not only books of polite literature, but histories without number, and all manner of treatises on science, are recorded in verse."

Physics, mathematics, and ethics; medicine, natural history, astronomy, and grammar, and even *cookery*, all lend themselves to verse in the East.

Amongst the most famous works of this kind is the *Kitáb Alághâni, or Book of Songs*, by Abu'lfaraj Ali Ben Hassayn Ben Mahomed Korashi Isfahani, who was born in the year of the Hegira 284. He was brought up at Bagdad, was deeply learned in the history of the Arabs, and in all other knowledge, and took his place with the most distinguished men of his time. He devoted fifty years to the composition of this, his celebrated work, and died in 356, having lost his reason some time previous to his death.

The Rose Garden of Persia

The *Kitáb Alághâni* is an important biographical work, notwithstanding its title, treating of grammar, history, and science, as well as poetry.

The work was unknown in France till it was discovered in the expedition to Egypt, and brought home by M. Raige. The manuscript he procured is now in the Royal Library: it consists of four folio volumes. M. Von Hammer is in possession of a copy. The basis is a collection of one hundred songs made for the Caliph Raschid: the airs are given, with commentaries and parallels. It may answer, in some respects, to our *Percy's Reliques*.

But it is with subjects purely poetical and imaginative that the present work has to do.

Who is there that is not familiar with those beautiful verses of Sir William Jones, translated from Hafiz?

"Sweet maid, if thou wouldst charm my sight," etc.

This learned man and elegant and accomplished poet once, as he informs us, proposed

Introduction

making a collection of Persian poetry, and giving it an English dress; if he had fortunately done so, and rendered the ideas as finely as he has done in the above poem, he would have made a valuable present to his country, for none could have executed the task so well; but his labours and avocations were too many and too various to admit of his performing the task he desired. No one, since his time, has attempted it, although numerous poems have been, from time to time, presented to the English reader; and Ferdusi and Sadi, in particular, have found their translators in learned and industrious scholars.

Atkinson, Chézé, and Von Hammer have in England, France, and Germany done much towards rendering the greatest Persian poets known; but a less learned hand may perhaps succeed in making them more familiar, and, by collecting a great number of poets together, enable the reader to judge and compare at his leisure. Not that it would be possible to offer specimens of one-quarter of the myriad poets of Persia!

The Rose Garden of Persia

So great has been my own delight and enthusiasm on the subject for many years, that I cannot help hoping that others may feel equally interested with myself, and happy to have found a new source of admiration of the graceful and beautiful.

I scarcely dare address a word to the Oriental scholar in extenuation of my attempt to render his darling poets into my northern tongue: I only trust he will forgive the boldness for the sake of the devotion, and, instead of being severe, will at once excuse the execution; considering only the motive which is to make "familiar in the mouth as household words" those unknown and unsought treasures, which he alone is capable of prizing to their full value.

To the Orientalist is known the extreme difficulty of conveying in any European tongue the exact meaning of the poet: the Germans have perhaps succeeded best, in consequence of the construction of their language; but mere *words* alone in Persian sometimes express so much that the translator finds all his efforts unavailing to render

Introduction

them of the same force. For instance, the Persians have words and names which at one view exhibit many qualities without more explanation, and which throw a charm over their songs, impossible to reach.

Such words as express *strewing-roses, emerald-hue, rose-cheeked, rose-lipped, jasmine-scented*, etc., save the poet infinite trouble, but are a great obstacle to the translator. Perhaps it is the very circumstance of endeavouring to render these ideas correctly which has cramped all who have tried to give versions of the Persian poets, so that almost the sole exceptions are the few poems given by Sir William Jones, in a manner unrivalled both for truth and sweetness.

Ferdusi's *Shah Namah*, the great epic, in an English garb, inspires as little admiration, as a whole, as any of the translators of the *Lusiad* do to an English reader: Professor Chézé's *Mejnûn and Leila*, elegant and interesting as the translation is, is yet somewhat tedious from its very correctness, and Sadi's fine poems, the *Bostân* and the *Gulistân*, though they have been well rendered in

The Rose Garden of Persia

English prose, are somewhat ineffective, and it requires the genius of Moore himself to translate adequately his brother minstrel, Hafiz. A few extracts only of these long poems are all I offer.

As I know little of the Persian poets in the original, and am generally indebted to the above, and other learned authors, who have furnished accurate translations, I am the more fearful of the success of my endeavour to make them popular, in spite of the *bonne volonté* I may bring to the task; but, I repeat, it has been one so very pleasing to me, that I cannot abandon the hope that the "Rose Garden of Persia," even in my hands, may not be considered without perfume.

ON ORNAMENT

The Orientals appear to agree in opinion with the Italians, that "molto cresce una beltà, uno bel manto"; for they have at all times taken great delight in adorning their manuscripts, considering that they thus do honour to the subject. Rousseau's feeling of paying proper homage to his manuscript Héloise would be thoroughly understood in the East.

The works of favourite poets are generally written on fine silky paper, the ground of which is often powdered with gold or silver dust; the margins are illuminated; and the whole perfumed with some costly essence. Amongst others, that magnificent volume containing the poem of Yussuf and Zuleika, preserved in the public library at Oxford, affords a proof of the honours accorded to poetical compositions: the British Museum

The Rose Garden of Persia

is also rich in equally beautiful manuscripts.

One of the finest specimens of calligraphy and illumination is the exordium to the *Life of Shah Jehan*, for which the writer, besides the stipulated remuneration, had *his mouth stuffed* with the most precious pearls.

A finely ornamented book is considered an excitement to youth to study: in the preface to a work called *The Dispelling of Darkness*, is this passage: "This work, accurately written for its calligraphy, must be a comfort and excitement to the young."

Calligraphy is called in the East "a golden profession." Of all books copied with peculiar care and taste, the Koran has employed the greatest number of writers, who vie with each other in their extraordinary performances in this style; this caused the poet Sadi to say that "the Koran was sent to reform the conduct of men, but men thought only of embellishing its leaves."

A maxim of Caliph Ali was, "Learn to write well; fine writing is one of the keys of riches."

On Ornament

The Persian commentator on *Arabic Aphorisms* (ed. Weston), says: "Words set to music have a wondrous power when aided by inspiration and the *magic of fine writing*." Again—"A poem is a sweet-scented flower, spotted like a leopard, polished with much rubbing, and *written with the ink of two centuries*." "An impostor rivets his triumph by *writing carelessly*, and making it difficult to decipher, so that no extracts can be made that will repay the loss of time in reading it."

Fakr-eddin Rasi, when speaking of the merits of the Caliph Mostasem-billah, says: "He knew the Koran by heart, and his handwriting was very beautiful."

A manuscript of the *Divan* of the poet Kemal, which had been the property of a sultan, is possessed by the Imperial Library at Vienna, and is a great treasure as a splendid specimen of fine writing, and also for the superbly executed miniatures which adorn it, illustrating the poems. These pictures are not more than a square inch in size: there are two on each side of the concluding verse, and, though so small, represent with the

The Rose Garden of Persia

greatest correctness, either allegorically or simply, the meaning of the poet.

Mr. Edward More, author of the *Hindoo Pantheon*, mentions some very exquisite manuscripts in his possession: one, of fourteen and a half feet long, can be rolled up to the size of a man's thumb. The library of the India House, and that of the Asiatic Society in London, from the latter of which I have been allowed to take patterns for this work, are rich in very beautiful specimens of Oriental minuteness: amongst them are copies of the Koran on delicate strips exquisitely illuminated, so small as to require a strong glass to decipher the character. Some of these can be rolled up into an almost incredibly small space and carried in the pocket. Nothing but the fairy's gift of tapestry, which could be enclosed in a walnut shell, can be compared to these wonders. A copy of the *Mahabarata* was lately in London, which is said to exceed all that could be imagined of human patience in the minute beauty of its execution.

The ink used in the East is extremely

On Ornament

black, and never loses its colour. Egyptian reeds, with which the scribes write, are formed to make the finest strokes and flourishes, and their letters run so easily into one another, that they can write faster than any other nation.

There is a beautiful manuscript of Dowlat Shah of Samarkand's valuable *Lives of the Persian Poets*, in the Royal Library at Paris.

THE SUFIS

Most of the Asiatic poets are *Sufis*, a profession of religion so mystical, that it is difficult to explain in a few words.

They prefer, or profess to prefer, the meditations and ecstasies of mysticism to the pleasures of the world. Their fundamental tenets are, that nothing exists *absolutely* but God: that the human soul is an emanation from His essence, and will finally be restored to Him: that the great object in this transitory state should be, a constant approach to the Eternal Spirit, and as perfect a union to the Divine nature as possible; for which reason all worldly attachments should be avoided, and, in all we do, a spiritual object should be kept in view—

"As a swimmer, without the impediment of garments, cleaves the water with greater ease."

The Sufis

When a Sufi poet speaks of love and beauty, a divine sentiment is always to be understood, however much the words employed may lead the uninitiated to imagine otherwise. This is the case with many sects of Protestants, and appears also in the sacred poems of our early writers, in those of the Fathers of the Church, and in the Song of Solomon, which is a remarkable instance.

The great end with these philosophers is to attain to a state of perfection in spirituality, so as to be at length totally absorbed in holy contemplation, to the exclusion of all worldly recollections or interests. This is, in fact, no more than was formerly sought by monastic devotees in the Catholic Church; and it was the same belief and endeavour which produced so many saints and martyrs.

As religious enthusiasm, carried to the utmost height, is sure to—

"O'erleap itself, and fall on the other side,"

the admirers of the Sufis carried their zeal beyond all bounds, and the *ultra* pious added

The Rose Garden of Persia

still greater mysticism to a belief which was already obscure enough. This has filled the deserts of India and Arabia with howling dervishes, *Yoghis*, *Sunnis*, and whole tribes of fanatics, who have run wild with ill-directed devotion, and pass their lives standing on one leg or ceaselessly extending one arm, or with fixed eyes constantly regarding the sun till they lose their sight. Such as these have made their faith a jest, and such are described as perfect beings by those of their own sect who encourage such absurdity.

In a work called *Exercise of the Soul*, they are named as follows, their wisdom and their folly lauded alike:—

"He is both a Yoghi and a Sunnyasi, who performeth that which he ought to do, independent of the fruit thereof. To the Yoghi gold, iron, and stone are the same. The Yoghi constantly exerciseth the spirit in private, free from hope, free from perception. He planteth his own seat firmly on a spot undefiled, neither too high nor too low, and sitteth upon the sacred grass, which

The Sufis

is called Koos, covered with a skin or a cloth. There he whose business is the restraining of his passions, should sit with his mind fixed on one object, alone, in the exercise of his devotion for the purification of his soul, *keeping his head, neck, and body steady, without motion,* his eyes fixed *on the point of his nose,* looking at no other place around."

When it is considered that the creed of the Sufis is to adore *beauty,* because the contemplation thereof leads the creature nearer to the Creator; and to venerate *wine,* because of the power of its spirit is a symbol of that of the Deity, the reader of the Persian poets will not be surprised at the mixture of sacred, and apparently profane, ideas so often found in the same poem.

Hafiz, himself a Sufi, has well expressed the sentiments of this visionary sect in the following lines, which will at once convey the substance of this mystical belief, so frequently and necessarily alluded to when the Persian poets are treated of:—

The Rose Garden of Persia

EARTHLY AND HEAVENLY LOVE

A MYSTICAL POEM OF HAFIZ

A being, formed like thee, of clay,
Destroys thy peace from day to day;
Excites thy waking hours with pain;
Consumes thy sleep with visions vain.
Thy mind is rapt, thy sense betrayed;
Thy head upon her foot is laid.
The teeming earth, the glowing sky,
Is nothing to her faintest sigh.

Thine eye sees only her; thy heart
Feels only her in every part.
Careless of censure, restless, lost,
By ceaseless wild emotions tost;
If she demand thy soul, 'tis given—
She is thy life, thy death, thy heaven.

Since a vain passion, based on air,
Subdues thee with a power so rare,
How canst thou marvel those who stray
Tow'rds the true path are led away,
Till, scarce the goal they can descry
Whelmed in adoring mystery?

The Sufis

Life they regard not ; for they live
In *Him* whose hands all being give :
The world they quit for *Him*, who made
Its wondrous light, its wondrous shade :
For *Him* all pleasures they resign,
And love *Him* with a love divine !

On the *cup-bearer* gazing still,
The cup they break, the wine they spill.
From endless time their ears have rung
With words, by angel voices sung ;
"Art thou not bound to God?" they cry ;
And the blest "Yes" whole hosts reply.

They seem unmoved, but ceaseless thought
Works in their minds, with wisdom fraught.
Their feet are earth, but souls of flame
Dwell in each unregarded frame.
Such power by steady faith they gain,
One yell would rend the rocks in twain ;

One word the cities could o'erthrow,
And spread abroad despair and woe.

The Rose Garden of Persia

Like winds, unseen, they rove all ways
Silent, like stone, they echo praise:
So rapt, so blest, so filled are they,
They know not night—they see not day

So fair *He* seems, all things who made,
The forms He makes to them are shade;
And, if a beauteous shape they view,
'Tis His reflection shining through.

The wise cast not the pearl away,
Charmed with the shell, whose hues are gay;
To him *pure love* is only known,
Who leaves *both worlds* for God alone.

It is necessary to explain, in some degree, the nature of the Sufi belief, in order that the reader, to become initiated, should not be startled at the singular expressions, which he is bound to comprehend as conveying a sacred meaning; otherwise, when the poet exclaims, in a mystical rapture—

"Sell this world *and the next for a cup of pure wine*!"

The Sufis

it might be imagined extraordinary, until he knows that by a "cup of pure wine" is meant "faith."

It must be confessed that the following ode of Hafiz requires to be studied with more than ordinary attention, in order that the full meaning of its *devotional* fervour may be comprehended; otherwise, it might appear to the *unguarded* reader a mere Bacchanalian effusion, not unworthy of Anacreon!

ODE OF HAFIZ

SAID TO BE EXPRESSIVE OF HOLY JOY AND EXULTATION

Grapes of pure and glowing lustre!
May the hand that plucked each cluster
    Never shake with age!
May the feet ne'er slip that press them!
Oh! 'tis rapture to possess them,
    'Spite the chiding sage.

The Rose Garden of Persia

Call, call for wine, the goblet drain,
  And scatter round spring's fairest flowers;
What wouldst thou more of fate obtain:
  Where canst thou seek for brighter hours?
This was the earthly nightingale's first lay;
What sayest thou to his precepts, Rose of Day?

Oh! bring thy couch where countless roses
The garden's gay retreat discloses;
There in the shade of waving boughs recline,
Breathing rich odours, quaffing ruby wine!

Thou, fairest rose of all, oh say,
For whom thy hundred leaves dost thou display?
To what blest mortal wilt thou own
Such buds have sprung for him alone?

The Sufis

What have I now to ask?—here all
    Life's choicest gifts to me belong;
Prudence and wisdom are but thrall,
    The only friends are wine and song!

The religion of the Sufis appears to be a compound of the philosophy of Plato and Berkley: with Plato, they would perfectly agree in the following observation: "For a thing of this kind cannot be expressed by words, like other disciplines, but by lasting familiarity and conjunction of life with this divine object, a bright light on a sudden, as it were, leaping out of a fire, will illuminate the soul, and then preserve and nourish its splendour." Or with Socrates: "There is but one eternal, immutable, uniform beauty, in contemplation of which our sovereign happiness does consist, and therefore a true lover considers beauty and proportion as so many steps and degrees by which he may ascend from the particular to the general; from all that is lovely in feature, or regular in proportion, or charming in sound, to the general fountain of all perfection. And if you are so much transported with the sight of beautiful persons as to wish neither to eat nor drink, but to pass your whole life in their conversation, to what ecstasy would it raise you to behold the original beauty, not filled up with flesh and blood, or varnished with a fading mixture of colours, and the rest of mortal trifles and fooleries, but separate, uniform, and divine!"

The Sufis suppose that it is an anxious desire of the soul for union that is the cause of love: thus they compare the soul to a bird confined in a cage, panting for liberty, and pining at its separation from the divine essence.

FAVOURITE SUBJECTS OF EASTERN POETS

There are three principal love-stories in the East, which, from the earliest times, have been the themes of every poet. Scarcely one of the mighty masters of Persian literature but has adopted and added celebrity to those beautiful and interesting legends,

The Sufis

which can never be too often repeated to an Oriental ear. They are,—"The History of Khosrû and Shireen"; "The Loves of Yussuf and Zuleika"; and "The Misfortunes of Mejnoun and Leila." So powerful is the charm attached to these stories, that it appears to have been considered almost an imperative duty on the poets to compose a new version of the old, familiar, and beloved traditions. Even down to a modern date, the Persians have not deserted their favourites, and these celebrated themes of verse reappear, from time to time, under new auspices.

Each of these poems is expressive of a peculiar character: that of Khosrû and Shireen may be considered exclusively the Persian romance; that of Mejnoun, the Arabian; and that of Yussuf and Zuleika, *the Sacred*. The first presents a picture of happy love and female excellence in Shireen. Mejnoun is a representation of unfortunate attachment, carried to madness. The third romance contains the ideal of perfection in Yussuf (*i.e.* Joseph), and the most passionate

The Rose Garden of Persia

and imprudent love in Zuleika (the wife of Potiphar); and exhibits in strong relief the power of love and beauty, the mastery of mind, the weakness of overwhelming passion, and the victorious spirit of holiness and triumph of prophecy—for it is said that Yussuf's beauty was foreshown to Adam as a type of his prophetic power. The names of three great poets are identified with these subjects; and each has peculiarly succeeded in one: to Nizami is accorded the palm, for the best poem on "The Loves of Khosrû and Shireen"; to Jami, for those of "Yussuf and Zuleika"; and to Hatifi, for the "*most* musical, *most* melancholy" version of the sad tale of "Mejnoun and Leila," the Romeo and Juliet of the East. These are generally called the Romantic Poets, as the others are the Mystic and the Historic.

The first of Persian poets, the father of his language, the Homer of his country, is the illustrious Ferdusi, whose name is known in every nation, and consecrated to eternal fame in his own. He is the head of the Historic school.

FERDUSI

When the renowned conqueror Shah Mahmoud reigned in Ghusni, supreme ruler of Zablistan and great part of Khorassan, he entertained several poets in his palace, amongst whom the most distinguished was Abul Kasim Mansûr, called *Ferdusi*, or "Paradise," from the exquisite beauty of his compositions. The poet had been attracted from his village by the fame of the sultan's magnificence; for he had spent fifty years of his life in his native place, Shadàb, in the province of Tûs, in Khorassan, without seeking reputation beyond. His name, however, had spread far and wide, and the sultan heard with pride that so great a luminary had come to shed its lustre over his court, which wanted but that to dazzle the whole world.

The gorgeous gates of sandal-wood, which

he had transported to his palace from the idol temple of Somnât, he thought alone worthy to expand to let in such a guest as Ferdusi; and the unrivalled city of palaces which he had created, in the midst of which stood the abode which he thought worthy of the name of "the Celestial Bride," he considered never so much honoured as when the "Minstrel of the Garden of Paradise" set his foot within its walls. Neither of his majestic Bala Hissar, the emblem of his power, nor of his glorious *minars*, which remain to this day memorials of his greatness, was Mahmoud more proud, than that Ferdusi was, by his command, composing, in his faultless verse, a history of the monarchs of Persia, his predecessors.

No reward then appeared to him too great to offer to induce the poet to undertake the task, no promises too splendid to excite him. "Write, unequalled one," cried he, "and for every thousand couplets a thousand pieces of gold shall be thine."

But Ferdusi wrote for fame and not for profit, though he was poor, and depended

Ferdusi

only on his own exertions; he resolved to accept of no reward till he had completed the work he had undertaken, and for *thirty years* he studied and laboured that his poem might be worthy of eternal fame. In this he succeeded, but the patience of the Shah was exhausted, his enthusiasm was gone, his liberality had faded away, and when the sixty thousand couplets of the *Shah Namah*, or "Book of Kings," was ended, there was a pause, which brought to the poet disappointment, and to the monarch such everlasting disgrace as has obliterated all his triumphs.

What must have been the poet's feelings, when, after a life of labour, of unabated enthusiasm, unwearied diligence, and undiminished zeal, though he had by this time reached the age of eighty years, he found the announcement of his great epic's completion coldly received! Incautious even more than is usual with his rhyming race was the hapless Ferdusi, to trust to the continuance of a king's patronage for so long a period. Enemies had thickened round him while he was absorbed in his great work, his friends had disappeared, his admirers had dropped off, and the unfortunate minstrel woke from his protracted dream to find himself

"A very beggar and a wretch indeed."

There is something that sounds like Eastern exaggeration in the term of years named, and the age of the poet, but all historians have so recounted the event. Thirty years is a long period to make a monarch and the public wait for a promised work, and it a little diminishes the pity which would be naturally felt for the author when the disappointment of the patron is considered.

Ferdusi sent a copy, exquisitely written, of his *Shah Namah* to the sultan, who received it unmoved: the grand vizier uttered deprecatory remarks, the courtiers yawned, and the aged poet's long-looked-for work was treated with contempt.

The astonished author of an unrivalled composition, of the value of which he was well assured, was startled at the silence of his royal patron; he began to reflect on his position, and the fact of his having for a

Ferdusi

series of years neglected all his worldly affairs in order to give himself up entirely to study became painfully evident. He could scarcely believe in the meanness and ingratitude which could thus neglect him: but still no notice was taken. At length the following lines reached the ear of Mahmoud, and he began to fear the poet's fire was not all extinct:—

'Tis said our monarch's liberal mind
Is, like the ocean, unconfined.
Happy are they who prove it so!
'Tis not for me that truth to know.
I've plunged within its waves, 'tis true,
But not a single pearl could view.

Shamed, piqued, and offended at this freedom, the sultan ordered sixty thousand small pieces of money (dirrhims) to be sent to the author of the *Shah Namah*, instead of the gold which he had won. Ferdusi was in the public bath at the time the money arrived, and his rage and amazement exceeded all bounds when he found himself thus insulted.

The Rose Garden of Persia

"How!" he exclaimed, "does the sultan imagine that thirty years' labour and study are to be rewarded with dirrhims?" So saying, he distributed the paltry sum amongst the attendants of the bath and the slave who brought it.

At first his mind was overwhelmed with grief and vexation; all the airy dreams he had formed of devoting the promised sum to the embellishment of his native place, endowing a hospital, and becoming a general benefactor to his province, were at once dispersed, and the fame for which he had toiled appeared to have vanished also; but in a short time his spirit rose superior to sorrow, and his former energy and dignity returned. He called up every feeling of contempt and bitterness of which his sensitive nature was capable, and resolved to pour the accumulated torrent on the head of the degraded sovereign who had deceived and insulted him. The circumstances of Mahmoud's birth left him open to contumely, for though his father, Sebectighin, rose to empire from his valour and brilliant qualities,

Ferdusi

there was a blot in his escutcheon not to be forgotten, particularly under such provocation—he had been a *slave*!

The excited poet relieved his mind by a satire full of stinging invective, and caused it to be transmitted to the favourite vizier who had instigated the sultan against him; it was carefully sealed up, with directions that it should be read to Mahmoud on some occasion when his mind was perturbed with affairs of state and his temper ruffled, as it was a poem likely to afford him entertainment. Ferdusi having thus prepared his vengeance, quitted the ungrateful court, without leave-taking, and he was safely arrived in Mazanderan when news reached him that his lines had fully answered the purpose he had intended they should do. Mahmoud had heard and trembled, and too late discovered that he had ruined his own reputation for ever.

There is in this celebrated satire a remarkable expression, singularly like that of Wolsey:—"Had I written as many verses in praise of Mahommed and Ali as I have

The Rose Garden of Persia

composed for King Mahmoud, they would have showered a hundred blessings upon me!"

The following is part of the satire:—

FERDUSI'S SATIRE ON MAHMOUD OF GUSNI

In Mahmoud who shall hope to find
One virtue to redeem his mind?
A mind no gen'rous transports fill;
To truth, to faith, to justice chill!
Son of a slave!—His diadem
In vain may glow with many a gem,
Exalted high in power and place,
Outbursts the meanness of his race!

Take, of some bitter tree, a shoot—
In Eden's garden plant the root;
Let waters from th' Eternal spring
Amidst the boughs their incense fling;
Though bathed and showered with honey dew,
Its native baseness springs to view;—

Ferdusi

After long care and anxious skill,
The fruit it bears is bitter still.

Place thou within the spicy nest,
Where the bright phœnix loves to rest,
A raven's egg—and, mark it well,
When the vile bird has chipped its shell,
Though fed with grains from trees that grow
Where Salsebil's sweet waters flow,
Though airs from Gabriel's wings may rise
To fan the cradle where he lies,
Though long these patient cares endure,
It proves, at last, a bird impure!

A viper, nurtured in a bed
Where roses all their beauties spread,
Though nourished with the drops alone
Of waves that spring from Allah's throne,
Is still a poisonous reptile found,
And with its venom taints the ground.

Bear, from the forest's gloom, to light,
The dark and sullen bird of night;

The Rose Garden of Persia

Amidst thy garden's sweetest bowers
Place him with summer's fairest flowers;
Let hyacinths and roses glow,
And round his haunts their garlands throw;
Scarce does the sun in glory rise,
And streak with gold the laughing skies,
He turns him from the day in pain,
And seeks his gloomy woods again.

This truth our holy Prophet sung—
"All things return from whence they sprung.
Pass near the merchant's fragrant wares,
Thy robe the scent of amber bears;
Go where the smith his trade pursues,
Thy mantle's folds have dusky hues.

Let not those deeds thy mind amaze
A mean and worthless man displays;
An Ethiop's skin becomes not white;
Thou canst not change the clouds of night.
What poet shall attempt to sing
The praises of a vicious king?

Ferdusi

Hadst thou, degenerate prince, but shown
One single virtue as thy own;
Had honour—faith—adorned thy brow,
My fortunes had not sunk, as now;
But thou hadst gloried in my fame,
And built thyself a deathless name.

O Mahmoud! though thou fear'st me not,
Heaven's vengeance will not be forgot;
Shrink, tyrant! from my words of fire,
And tremble at a poet's ire!

The only part of this invective which was undeserved was Ferdusi's allusion to the father of the sultan, who merited more from one who could appreciate virtue than to be merely named as "*a slave.*" What the character of Sebectighin was the following anecdotes will show:—

"He was at first only a private horseman in the service of the sultan whom he succeeded on the throne; and, being of an active and vigorous disposition, used to hunt every day in the forest. It happened once, when he was thus amusing himself, that he saw a deer grazing with her young fawn, upon which, spurring his horse, he seized the fawn, and, binding its legs, threw it across the saddle and turned his face towards home. When he had ridden a little way, he looked behind, and beheld the mother of the fawn following him and exhibiting every mark of extreme affliction. The soul of the hunter melted within him; he untied the feet of the fawn, and generously restored it to liberty. The happy mother turned towards the wilderness, and often looked back upon him, the tears dropping fast from her eyes. That night he saw an apparition in his dreams, which said to him, 'The kindness and compassion which thou hast this day shown to a distressed animal has been approved of in the presence of God; therefore in the records of Providence the kingdom of Ghusni is marked as a reward against thy name. Let not greatness destroy thy virtue, but continue thy benevolence to man.'"

It is related in a moral, metaphysical,

Ferdusi

and philosophical work, called *Masir ul Maluck*, that Mahmoud, when prince, having built a pleasure-house in an elegant garden, near the city of Ghusni, invited his father to a magnificent entertainment, which he had prepared for him. The son, in the joy of his heart, desired to know his father's opinion as to his taste in the structure which had been lauded as inimitable. The king, to the great disappointment of Mahmoud, told him "that he looked upon the whole as a bauble, which any of his subjects might have raised by means of wealth; but that it was the business of a prince to erect the more durable structure of good fame, which might stand for ever to be imitated, but never to be equalled."

The great poet Nizami makes, upon this saying, the following reflection: "Of all the gorgeous palaces that Mahmoud built we now find not one stone upon another, but the edifice of fame, as he was told by his father, still triumphs over time, and is established on a lasting foundation."

The Rose Garden of Persia

The *Shah Namah* contains the history of the kings of Persia, from the reign of the first king, Kaiûmers, to the death of Yesdijerd, the last monarch of the Sassanian race, who was deprived of his kingdom, A.D. 641–A.H. 21, by the invasion of the Arabs during the caliphate of Omar.

In the course of this period three dynasties sat upon the Persian throne. The first, called the Pishdadian, lasted 2441 years; the second, the Kaianian, commenced with Kai-kobád, and lasted 732 years. Alexander the Great (or Sikander) is included in this race, and is, by the poet, represented as the son of Dârab, king of Persia, by the daughter of Failakus (Philip of Macedon).

After the death of Sikander, Persia was divided, during 200 years, into a number of petty monarchies, called the "Confederacy of the kings." The Sassanian race of princes succeeded these, and ruled over Persia for 501 years.

As a history, the great poem of Ferdusi is now of little value; but it contains some

Ferdusi

of the ancient Persian traditions, and the power and eloquence of its verse are unrivalled.

Persian biographers all agree in asserting that Mahmoud placed in the hands of Ferdusi the ancient chronicles of the kings of Persia, from which it is supposed that he derived his historical narratives. That such fragments existed we have the testimony of the Book of Esther, besides those of Herodotus and Ctesius.

A story is often repeated respecting the origin of Ferdusi's work, which is perhaps founded on truth, but has been much doubted.

One book, besides the fables of Bidpai, or Pilpai, is said to have escaped from the burning of the Alexandrian library, namely, a history of Persia, in the *Pehlevian* or vulgar dialect, supposed to have been compiled by order of Nishurvan or Kosroës, who reigned till near the close of the sixth century. Saad, one of Omar's generals, found the volume, after the victory at Cadessia, and preserved it as a curiosity;

The Rose Garden of Persia

it passed through several hands, was translated into several dialects of Persia, and finally was seen by the great poet, who derived from it the materials of his poem.

After his satire had been read by Shah Mahmoud, the poet feared to remain too long in one place; he sought shelter in the court of the Caliph of Bagdad, Kadir Billah, in whose honour he added a thousand couplets to the *Shah Namah*, and who rewarded him with the sixty thousand gold dinars, which had been withheld by Mahmoud.

These lines occur amongst his compliments:—

TO THE KING

Nor vice nor virtue long endure,
Then keep thy conscience ever pure;
Wealth, power, and gorgeous works will seem
At the last hour an idle dream;
But a great name no time can steal:
Despise not then the sage's zeal.

Ferdusi

'Twas Feridoun, by Heav'n ordained,
Who first the world from vice restrained:
Great Feridoun, the blest and wise,
Was yet no child of paradise.
Not musk, or ambergris—but clay;
But truth and justice owned his sway:
Obedient, faithful, generous found,
His virtues by success were crowned:
Like him by virtue gain renown,
And reign another Feridoun.

Meantime Ferdusi's poem of *Jussuf*, and his magnificent verses on several subjects, had revived the fame which his studies had so long allowed to lie dormant, and Shah Mahmoud's "late remorse awoke." He had lost the greatest ornament of the age, and another monarch could boast of having done him right. He pretended to have discovered that his vizier had deceived him in attributing impiety to Ferdusi, and he at once sacrificed that favourite, dismissing him with disgrace. He had, however, previously sent to Kadir Billah to command the poet's absence from his court, and he had retired to his native Tûs. Thinking, by a tardy act of liberality, to repair his former meanness, Mahmoud despatched to the author of the *Shah Namah* the sixty thousand pieces he had promised, a robe of state, and many apologies and expressions of friendship and admiration, requesting his return, and professing great sorrow for their dissensions.

The poet, however, was " past the tyrant's stroke," and senseless of his future generosity. He was dead!—having expired in his native town, full of years and honours, surrounded by his friends and kindred.

His family, knowing his wishes, devoted the whole sum to the benevolent purposes he had intended, namely, the erection of public buildings, and the general improvement of the place of his birth. The date of his death is given as in A.D. 1020—A.H. 411, and his age as eighty-nine.

The language of Ferdusi may be considered as the purest specimen of the older Persian dialect, called *Deri*, Arabic words being rarely introduced ; whereas Sadi, Jami, Hafiz, and others have adopted Arabic ex-

Ferdusi

pressions without reserve. The softness of the *Deri*, in the opinion of the Asiatics, has occasioned the popular saying, "that it is the language of Heaven," together with the Arabic idioms. "God," it is said, "communicates His milder mandates in the delicate accents of the first, whilst His sterner commands are delivered in the rapid utterance of the other."

There are many episodes in the *Shah Namah* of great beauty. The following is the rhapsody of Byzun, a young prince, the *Paris* of Ferdusi's poem, who had reason to repent his adventure with the daughter of Afrasiab, for he was made captive, and only rescued by the valour of Rostam,—another *Rolando*, the great hero of the poem, of whom the most extraordinary feats are related, and who is, probably, the original of many of those who figure in the histories of knight-errantry.

The prince, sailing by the gardens of Afrasiab's palace, beholds his daughters wandering amidst the bowers, and, excited by a perfidious friend, forms the somewhat ungallant plan of carrying them off; he is thus addressed by his companion, Girgin, the traitor:

THE GARDENS OF THE DAUGHTERS OF AFRASIAB

FROM THE "SHAH NAMAH" OF FERDUSI

Look forth, companions, cast afar your eyes
  Where yonder many-coloured plain extends:
Ah! in my breast what sweet emotions rise!
  Behold how each soft charm of nature blends
Into one glorious whole,—grove, mead, and stream,—
A fit abode for heroes it might seem!

The tender silken grass invites the tread;
  With musky odour breathes the fanning air;
Pure waters glide along their perfumed bed,
  As though the rose gave them her essence rare;

Ferdusi

The lily stalk bends with her fragrant
 flower,
The lustre of the rose glads ev'ry bower.

The pheasant walks with graceful pace
 along,
  Soft doves and mournful nightingales
 are nigh,
Charming the silence with a mingled song,
  And murmurs from the cypress-boughs
 reply.

Oh! never, never,—long as time shall
 last,—
May shadows o'er these beauteous scenes
 be cast!
Still may they in eternal splendour glow,
And be like Paradise, as they are now!

There, in gay groups, beneath the trees,
 beside
Those streams that through the vales in
 music glide,
Lovely as fairies, beautiful as day,
Are maids who wander on in sportive play.

The Rose Garden of Persia

Afrasiab's daughter there, Manizha bright,
Makes the whole garden—like the sun—
 all light.

Not less majestic, 'midst the graceful
 throng,
Her sister, fair Zittara, sweet and young!
She decks the plain with beauty as she
 goes,
Before her shrink, ashamed, the jasmine
 and the rose!
And there are Turkish maids that near
 them rove,
With forms like cypress-boughs that
 zephyrs move;
Locks dark as musk,—and see! each veil
 discloses
Eyes *filled with sleep*, and cheeks all full
 of roses!

Shall we not, friends, turn for a single
 day,
Check, for so great a prize, our onward
 way,

Ferdusi

Steal to those bowers, make the bright
nymphs our own,
And bring the lovely prey to Khosrou's
throne?

Another episode of the *Shah Namah* relates the "loves of the Fair-haired Zal, or Zalzar, and Rudava." This hero is a very favourite one, as is his father, Sâm Nerimân, and his son is the famous Rostam, the conqueror of the Dives, or evil spirits. Rostam is the father of Sohrâb, an interesting young hero, whose tragical death is one of the most admired portions of the *Shah Namah*.

Another great hero of the *Shah Namah*, whose fabulous adventures are a favourite theme with Eastern writers, is Jamshid, the great monarch who owned the famous "jewel," so often named by the poets.

He is supposed to have flourished 800 years before the Christian era, and it was he who built "the famed Persepolis," or city of Istakar, the ruins of which, called Chelminar, or the Forty Pillars, still exist, and are often visited by adventurous travellers.

The Rose Garden of Persia

During his reign sickness and death were unknown, tranquillity and happiness rewarded the virtues of his people. The angel Siroush descended from heaven to visit the monarch, whose worth excited admiration in "both worlds," and a robe and enchanted girdle were left him by the celestial guest. He was gifted with a ray of divine light (like Moses), which rendered his form so luminous, that once, when descending Mount Alborz (from time immemorial the seat of fire-temples), the people imagined that there were two suns in the world. His magic *ring* and throne possessed extraordinary powers: his *goblet* was wondrous.

"Who knows," says the bard, "what is become of the goblet of Jam?"

He was beloved, feared, obeyed, and happy; but his human nature began at last to predominate over his better and more exalted feelings. Pride crept into his heart, and overturned the work of years: he became puffed up with self-estimation, and forgot from whence he derived his greatness,

Ferdusi

till the anger of God was kindled against him. The minds of his subjects underwent a change; they revolted, and drove him from his kingdom, and, an outcast and wanderer, he roamed the earth for a *hundred years*.

The following is a scene in which he is represented as meeting with the daughter of King Gureng, who became his wife; and, his probation past, he was restored to his kingdom and his power, "a wiser and a better man," his youth having suffered no diminution. The incidents and metaphors are from Ferdusi, but I have merely ventured on a *paraphrase*, not a translation.

JAMSHID'S COURTSHIP

A weary traveller sat to grieve
By Gureng's gate, at early eve,
Where fragrant gardens, filled with bloom,
Cast forth their breath of soft perfume,
And wandering o'er his brow and face,
Relieved him for a moment's space.

The Rose Garden of Persia

But sorrow weighed upon his breast,
    And dimmed the lustre of his eye;
He had no home—he sought but rest,
    And laid him down to sleep—or die!

  .   .   .   .   .

King Gureng's lovely daughter lies
    Beside a fountain gently playing;
She marks not though the waves be bright,
Nor in the roses takes delight:
And though her maids new games devise,
Invent fresh stories to surprise,
    She heeds not what each fair is saying:
Her fav'rite's voice has lost its spell,
The raven charms her ear as well!
But hark! soft whispers, questions gay,
    Amongst the female train prevail;
A young slave, beautiful as day,
    Blushes while she tells her tale.
"Nay, mock me not,—no face so fair
    Was seen on earth till now:
Though on his cheek are hues of care,
    And grief has marked his brow:
Ah! cruel maids, ye smile and doubt,
While the poor stranger faints without!"

Ferdusi

The princess heard: "Go hence," she cried,
"And be the stranger's wants supplied:
Let him beneath our shades repose,
And find a refuge for his woes."

The ready damsels straight obey,
And seek the trav'ller where he lay.
"Arise, fair youth, the wine-cup waits,
And roses bloom within our gates;
The tulip bids thee welcome be,
And the young moon has risen for thee."

Meanwhile the princess mused alone,
And thus she sighed in mournful tone:—
"Alas! they told me 'twas my fate;
But ah! I feel 'tis all too late:
I cannot now believe—'twas vain;
That dream can never come again!
And yet my nurse, who knows full well
Each herb and ev'ry potent spell,
From the cold wave can conjure fire,
And quell the mighty dragon's ire,
From stones soft dewdrops can distil,
And awe the *Dives* with wondrous skill;

The Rose Garden of Persia

Knows ev'ry star—has said that mine
Glowed with an aspect all divine;
That he, whose image is imprest,
As if by magic on my breast,
Whose portrait cheers my solitude—
The mighty Jamshid, great and good;
Of whose rare beauty they recount,
When he descended from the mount,
So bright the lustre, those who saw
Proclaimed two suns, and knelt in awe;
For whom the chains of death were riven,
Whom angels clothed in robes of heaven;
That prince whose power was far above
All those who vainly seek my love;
She said he should be mine—vain
    thought!
Is he not fall'n, to ruin brought;
His kingdom gone, his fortune crost,
And he, perhaps, for ever lost?"

She ceased, when lo! the laughing train
   Came dancing back with song and jest,
And leading, in a flowery chain,
   The stranger youth, their welcome guest.

Ferdusi

'Twas thus they met, they met and
    gazed,
Struck by the self-same power amazed;
Confused, admiring, pleased, distressed,
As passion rose in either breast.
The princess spoke, soft as a bird
   In spring to some dear partner sighing;
And the fair stranger's words were heard,
   Sweet as the *bul-bul's* notes replying.

Her long hair, streaming to the ground,
With odours fills the air around;
She moves to music and to song,
As the wild partridge steps along.

She leads him to her jasmine bower,
   'Midst fountains, birds, and blossoms
      sweet;
And her attendant maidens shower
   The sparkling wave upon his feet.
Two doves sat near, and softly mourned,
And both their hearts each sight returned.

With wine, and verse, and wit awhile,
The happy moments they beguile;

The Rose Garden of Persia

But clouds passed o'er the fair one's brow,
  She feared she doubted,—"Go!" she cried;
" Bring here my long-unbended bow,
  And let my former art be tried.
Two birds are seated on one tree,
Tell me which bird my mark shall be;
And thou shalt know a woman's skill
Can make all captive to her will!"

The stranger smiled with haughty look,
As from her hand the bow he took:
"Thy fame," he said, "to me is known;
Valour, like beauty, is thy own:
But know, though bold in camp and field,
Woman to man is forced to yield.
Princess, a boon! If I have wit
And skill the female bird to hit,
Shall she who makes these groves divine,
She whom I most admire, be mine?"

She blushed assent—the arrow flew;
  The female bird mounts to the skies;
His shaft has struck her pinions through,
  And fluttering on the ground she lies.

Ferdusi

The fair one's eyes with triumph shine:
  "The son of Tahúmers I see!
For never yet could hand but mine
  Bend that charmed bow—'tis he—'tis he!"

So spake her heart. "Give me the bow!"
  She said aloud; "if true my aim,
Let him who seeks me take me now,
  No better boon my hopes can claim."

My tale is told. Ye lovers, say,
  Can ye not guess the blissful close?
How Jamshid won a bride that day,
  And found a balm for all his woes.

Tahúmers, or Tahmúras, was a great hero, as well as his son; he received from the Simorgh (a fabulous Persian bird, of magical power) a present of some of her feathers, which is said to have given rise to the fashion of plumed helmets. This prince was called Banivand, *armed at all points*, and Diwband, chainer of Dives.

The mystics called the divinity *Simorgh*,

The Rose Garden of Persia

and *Anca*: mumerous fables are told of each, and they are sometimes said to be the same. There is a Persian saying, "All people have a proverb of the Anca, to express that which is spoken of and not seen." One poet, speaking of a miser, says, "His bread is like the Anca-Mogreb, which is painted on the carpet of kings, and of which men have made proverbs, but have never seen it. It is a figure which neither passes nor remains." M. Garcin de Tassy gives some curious notes on this extraordinary bird: "It is known only by name, and so called from having a white line round the neck like a collar; some say because of the *length of the neck* (this is not unlike the antediluvian wonders of geologists). It is said that the inhabitants of the city of Res had a prophet named Hantala, and there was in their country a mountain called Damaj, a mile high. There came there a very large bird, with a very long neck, of beautiful and divers colours. This bird was accustomed to pounce on all the birds of that mountain, and eat them up. One day he was hungry, and birds were scarce, so he pounced on a child,

Ferdusi

and carried it off; he is called Anca-Mogreb, because he carries off the prey he seizes. He afterwards pounced on a young girl, and putting her between his two smaller wings (for he has four on each side), bore her away. The people complained to their prophet, and he said, "My God, deliver us from this bird! prevent it from reproducing, and abandon it to misfortune."

Soon after this the Anca was struck with a thunderbolt. Mahomed is reported to have said, that at the time of Moses, God created a female bird called Anca; it had eight wings, *and bore the figure of a man*. God gave it a portion of everything, and afterwards created it a male. "Then God made this revelation to Moses (to whom be peace), I have created two extraordinary birds, and have assigned for their nourishment the wild beasts which are round Jerusalem. I have made you familiar with them, and I have given them over and above what I have accorded to the children of Israel."

But the species multiplied; and when Moses was dead they went to the land

The Rose Garden of Persia

of Najd and Hejaz, and never ceased to devour the wild beasts, and to carry off children, till the time when Khaled, son of Sénan Abasi, was prophet, between the time of Christ and Mahomed. It was then that these birds were complained of. Khaled invoked God, and God did not permit them to multiply, and their race became extinct.

Although Ferdusi holds the first place amongst the poets of Persia, he has himself mentioned that he is indebted for some passages in his historical poem to two poets who lived before him. These are Roduki and Dukiki, who appear to have both commenced a poetical version of the history of Persia. Of Roduki he speaks with respect, but criticises the other without mercy, although he condescended to adopt much of his composition.

It is related of Roduki, that the prince under whom he lived, having removed his court from Bokhara to Herât, became so attached to the latter city that he delayed his return, much to the regret of his courtiers, who employed the powers of the

Ferdusi

poet to induce the monarch to give up his new passion, and restore them to their homes and friends. Roduki fully entered into their views, and the following verses, sung with great feeling to the *barbut*, or viol, on which instrument he was a skilful performer, accomplished the end desired, and the prince, Umir Nussar, once again took the route to Bokhara.

THE REGRETS OF BOKHARA

The gale, whose breath such joy imparts,
   Comes from that gentle stream
Where they reside, to whom our hearts
   Return in mem'ry's dream:
The precious odour that its wings convey
Is their regret for us—so far away!

The sands are rough along that shore
   Where glides our native Amû's stream;
But when we tread its banks once more,
   Like velvet those rude sands will seem.

The Rose Garden of Persia

O pitying Oxus! let thy waves divide,
And yield us passage down thy opening tide!

All hail, Bokhara, land of flowers!
  Our prince moves proudly on;
He goes to glad thy sunny bowers,
  He asks thy smile alone.
The waving cypress seeks his native groves,
The rising moon the firmament it loves.

ESSEDI OF TÛS

Essedi of Tûs, in Khorassan, is distinguished as having been the master of the great Ferdusi. He held the first place as poet at the court of the Shah Mahmoud of Ghusni, until his fame was eclipsed by the lustre of that of his celebrated pupil. The Shah had several times required of Essedi to arrange the historical record of kings, which he declined, pleading his great age and the labour of so extensive an undertaking; he, however, recommended the execution of this important work to Ferdusi. When the latter, after his many cares and wanderings, returned to his native province of Tûs, his health having failed him, he feared that the end of his career was approaching, and he reflected with infinite pain that his immortal *Shah Namah* was uncompleted. To his aged master the

The Rose Garden of Persia

illustrious pupil communicated his sorrow, and his fears that no poet after him would put the finishing hand to his task. Essedi, in order to afford him comfort, assured him that should he survive he would devote himself to the performance of that duty.

"But alas! my master," said the desponding Ferdusi, "you are already very aged—how then will you be able to do this?"

"If it please God," answered the aged poet, "I shall complete it." At these words he quitted his pupil, and in the course of that night and the following day he composed no less than four thousand verses, thus concluding the great epic poem which conferred immortality on his beloved pupil, to whom he triumphantly brought his work; and so much was he amazed, gratified, and enchanted, that his health and spirits revived, and death was for a time averted.

Essedi must have been extremely aged when he achieved this extraordinary triumph, for the work itself had been declined by him, in the first place, on account of his advanced years, and no less than thirty of

Essedi of Tûs

his pupil's life had been passed in its composition.

The most celebrated of the other works of Essedi is his dispute between Day and Night.

Day and Night, who each can yield
   Joy and solace to the earth,
Thus contended for the field,
   Claiming both the highest birth—
Night spoke frowningly: "'Twas I
Who from all eternity
Ruled the chaos of the world,
When in dim confusion hurled.
The fervent prayer is heard at night;
Devotion flies day's glaring light.
'Twas night, the Mount when Moses left
   At night was Lot avenged by fire:
At night the moon our prophet cleft,
   And saw Heaven's might revealed entire.
The lovely moon for thirty days
   Spreads radiant glory from afar:
Her charms for ever night displays,
   Crowned, like a queen, with many a star:

The Rose Garden of Persia

Her seal-bearer is Heav'n, a band
Of planets wait on her command.
Day can but paint the skies with blue,
Night's starry hosts amaze the view.

Man measures time but by the moon;
Night shrouds what day reveals too soon.
Day is with toil and care oppressed,
Night comes, and with her, gentle rest.
Day, busy still, no praise can bring,
All night the saints their anthems sing;
Her shade is cast by Gabriel's wing!

The moon is pure, the sun's broad face
Dark and unsightly spots deface:
The sun shines on with changeless glare,
The moon is ever new and fair."

Day rose, and smiled in high disdain:
'Cease all this boasting, void and vain;
The Lord of heaven, and earth, and thee,
  Gave me a place more proud than thine,
And men with joy my rising see,
  And hail the beams that round me shine.

Essedi of Tûs

The holy pilgrim takes by day
To many a sacred shrine his way;
By day the pious fast and pray;
And solemn feasts are held by day.

On the *last day* the world's career is run,
As on the *first* its being was begun.

Thou, Night, art friendly, it may be,
For lovers fly for help to thee.
When do the sick thy healing see?

Thieves, by thy aid, may scathless prowl;
Sacred to thee the bat and owl;
And, led by thee, pale spectres grimly
    howl!

I sprang from heaven, from dust art thou:
    Light crowns my head with many a
        gem,
The collier's cap is on thy brow—
    For thee a fitting diadem.

My presence fills the world with joy:
Thou com'st all comfort to annoy.

The Rose Garden of Persia

I am a Moslem—white my vest:
Thou a vile thief, in sable drest.
Out, negro-face!—dar'st thou compare
Thy cheeks with mine, so purely fair?
Those 'hosts of stars,' thy boast and
    pride,
How do they rush their sparks to hide,
How to their native darkness run,
When, in his glory, comes the sun!

True, death was *first*; but, tell me, who
Thinks life least worthy of the two?
'Tis by the moon the Arab counts;
    The lordly Persian tells his year
By the bright sun, that proudly mounts
    The yielding heavens, so wide and clear.

The sun is ruddy, strong, and hale;
The moon is sickly, wan, and pale.
Methinks 'twas ne'er in story told
That silver had the worth of gold!
The moon, a slave, is bowed and bent,
She knows her light is only lent;
She hurries on, the way to clear,
Till the great Shah himself appear.

Essedi of Tûs

What canst thou, idle boaster, say
To prove the night excels the day?
If stubborn still, let Him decide
With whom all truth and law abide;
Let Nasur Ahmed, wise as great,
Pronounce, and give to each his state

UNSURI

It is related that, soon after the illustrious Ferdusi came into Persia, it happened on a certain day that Unsuri was sitting on the banks of a river with two companions, the poets Firoki and Asjudi, when, seeing a stranger approach whose dress had nothing distinguished in its appearance, they agreed amongst themselves to puzzle the new-comer and be merry at his expense. They proposed to recite three lines of poetry, each taking one line, and to demand the fourth of the stranger, who, in case of failure, was not to be permitted to remain in their society. Unsuri was the first to address Ferdusi (for it was no other) in an uncourteous tone, with the remark that none but poets should seek the company of poets; to which his future master modestly replied, "I also know a little of poetry." Unsuri then rose, and

Unsuri

recited the first line of a stanza, as agreed on :—

The moon, my fair, is pallid where thou art,

Asjudi continued :—

The colours of the rose to thine are pale;

Firoki went on :—

Thine eye can pierce, through armour, to the heart:

The three poets here paused, and, with contemptuous glances, desired the stranger to supply the concluding line, convinced that they required an impossibility from an obscure and probably unlearned person; but Ferdusi, without hesitation, instantly finished the verse thus :—

As Giû's swift arrow shivered Poshun's mail.

Not only were the three poets astonished at his readiness, but ashamed of their incivility,

The Rose Garden of Persia

and also of their inability to understand the allusion in the line of their conqueror, who explained it by reciting to them, now become attentive listeners, several parts of the *Shah Namah*, with which they were delighted, and Unsuri found that in the contemned stranger was a mighty master, whose genius had already created the work which Sultan Mahmoud had proposed to himself, having chosen him from seven contemporaries.

From this period contempt was changed to respect and admiration, nor did jealousy of his great rival ever find a place in the breast of the generous poet.

TOGRAY

TOGRAY was a native of Ispahan, and became so celebrated as a writer, that the title of "Honour of Writers" is sometimes given him: he was engaged in a chancellor's office, whose business it is to trace, in large characters, on the diplomas, the peculiar cypher, called Togray, generally written in a fine ornamented hand. This esteemed accomplishment, in which the poet excelled, was one of the causes of the enmity of Sultan Mahmoud's vizir, the same who was the enemy of Ferdusi.

Togray was vizir to the sultan of Moussûl, who was conquered by Mahmoud, and, being taken, the poet was put to death, from envy, by the rival vizir. A short time before, he had written some lines on the birth of a son, which show what his age was at the period:—

"This child, born to me in my old age,

has charmed my eyes, and inspired me, at the same time, with grave reflections, for *fifty-seven* years leave traces on the face of the hardest stone."

A collection of the poems of Togray has been made, the most celebrated of which is that called Lamiya-al-ajem, so called because all the verses terminate with the letter *lam*; the Persian *al-ajem* is added to distinguish it from an ancient poem of the same name, by another author.

The poet was addicted to alchemy, and wrote a treatise on the philosopher's stone.

EULOGY ON KASHMEER

Hail to the city from whose bowers—
The glowing paradise of flowers!—
Soft zephyrs waft the rose's breath,
  By moonlit night and blushing morn,
Even to the ruby, hid beneath
  The golden hills of Badakhshân!
Whose gale with perfume-laden wing,
O'er Arab deserts hovering,

Togray

A tint as radiant can bestow
As beams that in the emerald glow.

Upon thy mountains fresh and green
The velvet turf is scarcely seen,
So close the jasmines twine around,
And strew, with starlike flowers, the ground,
The ruddy glow of sunset lies
Within thy rich pomegranate's eyes;
And flashing 'midst the tulip-beds,
A blaze of glory round them sheds.

Night dwells amidst thy spicy groves;
Thy saffron fields the star of morning loves;
Thy violets have tales of eyes as fair;
Thy hyacinths of waving, dusky hair;
Thy glittering sunflowers make the year all spring;
Thy bees their stores are ever gathering;
And from the rose's branches, all day long,
Pours the melodious nightingale her song;
Amidst the leaves her barklike nest is tost,
In melody, and love, and beauty lost.

The Rose Garden of Persia

The rich narcissus, quaffing dewy wine,
Clings to thy breast, where buds unnumbered twine;
No eye can see the bound where end thy bowers,
No tongue can number half thy gem-like flowers.

Such freshness lingers in thy air of balm,
   That even the tulip's burning heart confesses
The life its sigh bestows at ev'ning's calm,
   When the glad cypress shakes her graceful tresses.

The waves of each rejoicing river
Murmur melody for ever,
And to the sound, in wild amaze,
On their glad crests the dancing bubble plays;
While lotus flowers, just opened, there
Look with bright eyes towards heaven in prayer.

So clear thy waters, that, reflected bright
The dusky Ethiop's skin is pearly white.

Togray

So cool, that as the sun his fingers laves,
They shiver on the surface of thy waves.
The immortal lily, pure as angels' plumes,
All day, all night, the grove with light illumes;
The grove, where garlands, by the roses made,
Like clustering Pleiads, glimmer through the shade,
And hide amidst their leaves the timid dove,
Whose ringèd neck proclaims the slave of love.

Tell me what land can boast such treasures?
  Is aught so fair, is aught so dear?
Hail! Paradise of endless pleasures!
  Hail! beautiful, beloved Kashmeer!

MOASI, KING OF POETS

Moasi rose from a low station, by the brilliancy of his genius, to become the favoured minstrel of a great king, and to have riches and honours showered upon him. His fame spread far and wide in the East, and he has been by some pronounced as inferior to no poet of his time. It was at the court of Melek Shah, of Ispahan, about the middle of the eleventh century A.D., that he became celebrated, and received the designation of King of Poets and the dignity of an emir. Khakani made him his model in versification; and so renowned were his odes, that more than a hundred poets endeavoured to imitate his style.

Moasi was sent by his patron on a mission to Constantinople, and is said to have returned from thence laden with presents of rich stuffs and a train of camels; he seems

Moasi, King of Poets

to have been more fortunate than most of his fellow-bards in keeping the favour of the prince who befriended him, for there are no vicissitudes recorded in his life.

The sultan was one evening on the terrace of his palace looking for the new moon, together with many of his nobles; the royal eyes were the first to perceive the appearance of the luminary, when he immediately commanded his poet to extemporise something on the occasion. Moasi, without hesitation, thus exclaimed:—

Thou moon, that gild'st the azure sphere,
  Art thou the fair one's lovely brow?
Or the rich jewel in her ear?
  Or the gold hoop of heaven, art thou?
Or art thou placed all earth to awe—
An arch of triumph for the Shah?

He was attached to the mysticism of the Sufis, like almost all the great poets, and his poems generally breathe the same spirit which animates them.

The Rose Garden of Persia

MYSTICAL ODE

What are both worlds but the sign
   That presents Almighty Love?
What are beauty's rays divine,
   But the beams that round Him move?

Since the floods flow from the sea,
   Let the river swell with pride;
Scarce a river can it be,
   'Tis itself the ocean tide.

When the small seed springs from earth,
Leaves, and bark, and fruit have birth;
But the tree so stately grown,
Was and is a grain alone.

Place thyself, oh, lovely fair!
Where a thousand mirrors are;
Though a thousand faces shine,
'Tis but one—and that is thine.

Then the painter's skill allow,
Who could frame so fair a brow.

Moasi, King of Poets

What are lustrous eyes of flame,
What are cheeks the rose that shame,
What are glances wild and free,
Speech, and shape, and voice—but He?

MYSTICAL ODE

Oh, behold the fair!—again
　Gaze upon them as they glide,
For their glances can explain
　Secrets hid from all beside.
Beauty first was sent to earth
But to give devotion birth;
And Moasi gazes on
Till his sense and rest are gone.
He is sunk and given up
To those eyes, and to the cup.

Since that radiant form passed by,
Writhed, like twisted locks, I lie;
And, like wheels that waters turn,
Now I groan, and sigh, and burn.
I am lost—so frail and weak!
Vainly for myself I seek.

The Rose Garden of Persia

In the east I saw a star,
Which allured me from afar;
And I gave my life to gaze,
Though I perish in its blaze.

Beauty! source of joy and pain;
  Beauty! that no words can speak;
Mejnoun's eyes must fixed remain
  On the rose of Leila's cheek.
And in Love's great empire where
Is a face so heavenly fair?
When I look on thee, no more
Eden tempts me with its store;
And the Tuba vainly throws
O'er the scene her perfumed boughs.
I a Paradise can own
When I gaze on thee alone.

Lo! I die, and carry hence
Nought of profit nor offence;
After life's brief toil is past,
I am base and poor at last.
When both worlds I thus resign,
Why should hell or heaven be mine?

Moasi, King of Poets

Who shall read his future lot?
I am blind, and see it not.
On the board Moasi traced
But two lines—how soon effaced!
They his destiny may show,
But their meaning who shall know?

KHAKANI

Khakani delighted in solitude, like his fellow-pupil Feleki, but, having absented himself from court without permission in order to enjoy it, he was pursued by order of Manucheher, and confined for seven months in the fortress of Schabran, where he had frequent conversations with certain captive Christians, and wrote a poem in praise of Christianity. Nevertheless, after his release he made a pilgrimage to Mecca, and wrote a *kassideh* on the journey, in which he describes the perils of the desert.

There is an odd story told of him and his patron, who appears to have been a dangerous person to deal with. The poet sent a letter to the prince requesting a present of a *lynx*, or *a hive of bees*: at which the patron was so much offended, that he should have the boldness to fetter his generosity

Khakani

with an *or*, that he sent an order for him to be *instantly put to death*.

The terrified bard, to screen himself, threw the blame on a fly smeared with honey, which, he said, had blotted the point under the word *with* (*ba*), and made it (*ya*), *or*, insisting that he had begged for a lynx *and* a hive of bees also. The ingenious expedient succeeded, and he escaped.

His death took place at Tabriz, A.D. 1186 (A.H. 582). He is considered the most learned of the lyric poets of Persia.

The following is curious, from the repetition at the end of each stanza: the poet seems in love with an unknown beauty:—

GAZEL

O waving cypress! cheek of rose!
  O jasmine-breathing bosom! say,
Tell me each charm that round her glows;
  Who are ye that my heart betray;
Tyrant unkind—to whom I bow,
O life-destroyer!—who art thou?

The Rose Garden of Persia

I saw thy form of waving grace,
   I heard thy soft and gentle sighs;
I gazed on that enchanting face,
   And looked in thy *narcissus* eyes;
Oh! by the hopes thy smiles allow,
Bright soul-inspirer—who art thou?

Where'er she walks, amidst the shades,
   Where perfumed hyacinths unclose,
Danger her ev'ry glance pervades—
   Her bow is bent on friends and foes.
The rich cheek shames the rose—thy brow
Is like the young moon—who art thou?

Thy poet-slave has dared to drain
   Draughts of thy beauty, till his soul,
Confused and lost in pleasing pain,
   Is fled beyond his own control.
What bliss can life accord me now
But once to know thee!—who art thou?

OMAR KHIAM

OMAR was one of the most remarkable, as well as the most distinguished, of the poets of Persia, at the latter end of the twelfth century. He was altogether unprecedented in regard to the freedom of his religious opinions—or, rather, his boldness in denouncing hypocrisy and intolerance, and the enlightened views he took of the fanaticism and mistaken devotion of his countrymen. He may be called the Voltaire of Persia, though his writings are not calculated to shock European notions so much as those of the followers of the Prophet. The priests were his great enemies, and he was peculiarly hated by the false devotees, whose arts he exposed. His indulgence to other creeds gave great offence, and his liberty of speech drew down upon him continued censure; yet was he extremely popular, and his composi-

The Rose Garden of Persia

tions were read with avidity by those who were not bigots, and the admiration of this class consoled him for the enmity of the other.

He was born at Nishapour, and devoted much of his time to the study of astronomy, of which science he was a learned professor; but it is asserted by his ill-wishers, that instead of his studies leading him to the acknowledgment of the power of the Supreme Being, they prompted him to disbelief. The result of his reflections on this important subject is given in a poem of his, much celebrated, under the title of Rubajat Omar Khiam.

He was the friend of Hassan Sabah, the founder of the sect of the Assassins; and it has been conjectured, assisted him in the establishment of his diabolical doctrines and fellowship. Some allowance must, however, be made for the prejudices of his historians, who would, of course, neglect nothing calculated to cast odium on one so inimical to their superstitions.

Omar Khiam seems particularly to direct

Omar Khiam

his satire against the mysticism of Moasi, and the rest of the Mystic Poets.

The following will give an idea of his compositions:—

PROFESSION OF FAITH

Ye who seek for pious fame,
And that light should gild your name,
Be this duty ne'er forgot,—
Love your neighbour—harm him not.
To Thee, Great Spirit, I appeal,
Who canst the gates of truth unseal;
I follow none, nor ask the way
Of men who go, like me, astray;
They perish, but Thou canst not die,
But liv'st to all eternity.
Such is vain man's uncertain state,
A little makes him base or great;
One hand shall hold the Koran's scroll,
The other raise the sparkling bowl—
One saves, and one condemns the soul.

The temple I frequent is high,
A turkis-vaulted dome—the sky,
That spans the worlds with majesty.

The Rose Garden of Persia

Not quite a Moslem is my creed,
Not quite a Giaour; my faith, indeed,
May startle some who hear me say,
I'd give my pilgrim staff away,
And sell my turban, for an hour
Of music in a fair one's bower.
I'd sell the rosary for wine,
Though holy names around it twine.
And prayers the pious make so long
Are turned by me to joyous song;
Or, if a prayer I should repeat,
It is at my beloved's feet.

They blame me that my words are clear;
Because I am what I appear;
Nor do my acts my words belie—
At least, I shun hypocrisy.
It happened that but yesterday
I marked a potter beating clay.
The earth spoke out—"Why dost thou strike?
Both thou and I are born alike;
Though some may sink, and some may soar,
We all are earth, and nothing more."

Omar Khiam

His verses in praise of beauty and wine are much esteemed:—

GAZEL

Nature made me love the rose,
  And my hand was formed alone
Thus the wine-cup to enclose;
Blame then—ye, the goblet's foes—
  Nature's fault, and not my own.
When a Houri form appears,
Which a vase of ruby bears,
Call me Giaour if then I prize
All the joys of Paradise!

IN PRAISE OF WINE

Morn's first rays are glimmering,
  From the skies the stars are creeping;
Rouse, for shame, the goblet bring,
  All too long thou liest sleeping:
Open those narcissus eyes,
Wake—be happy—and be wise!

The Rose Garden of Persia

Why, ungrateful man, repine,
When this cup is bright with wine?
All my life I've sought in vain
Knowledge and content to gain;
All that Nature could unfold,
Have I in her page unrolled;
All of glorious and grand
I have sought to understand.
'Twas in youth my early thought,
Riper years no wisdom brought,
Life is ebbing, sure though slow,
And I feel I nothing know.

Bring the bowl! at least in this
Dwells no shadowed distant bliss;
See; I clasp the cup whose power
Yields more wisdom in an hour
Than whole years of study give,
Vainly seeking how to live.
Wine disperses into air
Selfish thoughts and selfish care.
Dost thou know why wine I prize?
He who drinks all ill defies,
And can awhile throw off the thrall
Of self, the god we worship—all!

Omar Khiam

THE VANITY OF REGRET

Nothing in this world of ours
   Flows as we would have it flow;
What avail, then, careful hours,
   Thought and trouble, tears and woe?
Through the shrouded veil of earth,
   Life's rich colours gleaming bright,
Though in truth of little worth,
   Yet allure with meteor light.
Light is torture and suspense;
Thought is sorrow—drive it hence!
With no will of mine I came,
With no will depart the same.

THE CUP

Know'st thou whence the hues are drawn
Which the tulip's leaves adorn?
'Tis that blood has soaked the earth,
Where her beauties had their birth.

Know'st thou why the violet's eyes
Gleam with dewy purple dyes?

The Rose Garden of Persia

'Tis that tears, for love untrue,
Bathed the banks where first she grew.

If no roses bloom for me,
Thorns my only flowers must be :
If no sun shine on my way,
Torches must provide my day.
Let me drink, as drink the wise :
Pardon for our weakness lies
In the cup—for Heaven well knew,
  When I first to being sprung,
I should love the rosy dew,
  And its praise would oft be sung.
'Twere impiety to say
We would cast the cup away,
And be votaries no more,
Since it was ordained before.

    The latter part of the poem seems intended to ridicule the belief in predestination, carried to so absurd an extent by Mohammedans in general. Reland cites these lines on the subject :—

That which is written must arrive ;
'Tis vain to murmur or to strive :

Omar Khiam

Give up all thoughts to God, for He
Has fixed thy doom by His decree:
All good, all ill, depends on fate,—
The slaves of God must bear — and wait.

This belief in predestination extends to every created thing, not being confined to man alone. Sadee relates, in his *Gulistan*, a story of a fisherman, who had caught a fish which his strength did not allow him to drag to shore. Fearing to be drawn into the river himself, he abandoned his line, and the fish swam away with the bait in his mouth. His companions mocked him, and he replied: "What could I do? This animal escaped because his last hour, fixed by fate, was not yet come. Fate governs all, and the fisherman cannot overcome it more than another, nor can he catch fish, if fate is against him, even in the Tigris. The fish itself, *even though dry*, would not die, if it was the will of fate to preserve its life." The poet adds: "O man! why shouldst thou fear? If thy hour is not come, in vain would thy enemy rush against thee with his lance in rest: his arms and his feet would be tied by fate, and the arrow would be turned away, though in the hands of the most expert archer."

A father is made thus to speak to his son: "Honours and riches are not the fruits of our efforts, therefore give thyself no useless trouble; they cannot be obtained by force, and all efforts are of no more service than collyrium on the eyes of the blind. Thou mayest be a prodigy of genius, but all thy acquirements are of no avail if *fate is against thee.*"

A poet's version of the same idea runs thus:—

Reproach me not, and vainly say—
"Why idly thus, from day to day,
Let every good pass by thy door,
Nor swell by industry thy store?"
I answer,—labour, toil, and pain,
Prudence, wit, foresight,—all is vain.
Travels are useless: some succeed,
But others but to failure lead.

Omar Khiam

Fate rules—the miser counts his heaps,
And Fortune crowns him whilst he sleeps!

The poem which follows, by Omar Khiam, is in a strain of philosophy of a higher order.

THE WISDOM OF THE SUPREME

    All we see—above, around—
    Is but built on fairy ground:
    All we trust is empty shade
    To deceive our reason made.
    Tell me not of Paradise,
    Or the beams of houris' eyes;
    Who the truth of tales can tell
    Cunning priests invent so well?
    He who leaves this mortal shore
    Quits it to return no more.

    In vast life's unbounded tide
       They alone content may gain
    Who can good from ill divide,
    Or in ignorance abide—
       All between is restless pain.

The Rose Garden of Persia

Before Thy prescience, Power divine,
What is this idle sense of mine?
What all the learning of the schools?
What sages, priests, and pedants?—
 Fools!

The world is Thine, from Thee it rose,
By Thee it ebbs, by Thee it flows.
Hence, worldly lore! By whom is wisdom
 shown?
The Eternal knows, knows all, and *he*
 alone!

AZZ' EDDIN ELMO-CADESSI

FLOWERS AND BIRDS

Learn from birds and flowers, O man,
   Virtues that may gild thy name;
And their faults, if thou wouldst scan,
   Know thy failings are the same:
The fair narcissus, humble still,
   Reflecting on her lowly birth,
And feeling Nature, prone to ill,
   Inclines her soft eyes to the earth.

The water-lily, pale with care,
   Mourns as the waters pass her by;
"Alas!" she sighs, "what woes I bear!
   And must submit to misery:
But time can never teach my heart
From love's delusive joy to part!"

The Rose Garden of Persia

The willow is the only tree
  Whose slender boughs for ever wave;
Devotion in their homage see
  To Him who leaves and blossoms gave
And love that gentle willow knows,
Bending its glances towards the rose.

The modest jasmine is content,
She whispers, "Lovers, why lament?"

The bright anemone to view
Is bright and fair in shape and hue;
But in her leaves no perfume dwells,
  And in her heart is wickedness:
With secret scorn her bosom swells;
  Her crimes upon her mem'ry press:
"Behold," she muses, "beauty glows,
  All radiant in each outward part;
But ah! my soul too sadly knows
  That vice is burning in my heart!

Thou see'st the nightingale in spring—
  He seems as joy were all his own—
From tree to tree, with rapid wing,
  He flits, with love in ev'ry tone;

Azz' Eddin Elmocadessi

So volatile, so debonair,
As though he never knew a care.
But ah! how much art thou deceived!
   His heart is filled with pensive pain,
For earth's frail lot his soul is grieved;
   He sees her glory's fleeting train,
And how each beauty withers fast,
Nor leaves a shadow where it passed.
He knows that ruin soon will seize
The sweetest flowers, the fairest trees;
He knows the garden will decay,
And marks it fading day by day.
Thus, if aright thou read his song,
It tells of grief the whole year long!

Know'st thou why round his neck the dove
   A collar wears?—it is to tell
He is the faithful slave of love,
   And serves all those who serve him well.

The swallow leaves his lowly nest,
   And hies him to a foreign shore:
He loves with courtly man to rest,
   From whom he learns a higher lore

The Rose Garden of Persia

Than if he kept amongst his kind,
Nor sought with care to store his mind.
And men the welcome swallow prize,
    For he a kindly guest is known;
No base or selfish end he tries,
    But friendly converse seeks alone.

The owl has learnt the world's deceit,
    Its vanity and struggles vain;
And deems it flattery unmeet,
    A thought from reason to obtain.
Apart from the perfidious throng,
    In wisdom's contemplative mood,
To Heaven she gives her whole life long,
    And steals to holy solitude.

The peacock, wedded to the world,
    Of all her gorgeous plumage vain,
With glowing banners wide unfurled,
    Sweeps slowly by in proud disdain;
But in her heart a torment lies,
That dims the lustre of those dyes;
She turns away her glance—but no,
Her hideous feet appear below!

Azz' Eddin Elmocadessi

And fatal echoes, deep and loud,
   Her secret mind's dark caverns stir;
She knows, though beautiful and proud,
   That Paradise is not for her.
For, when in Eden's blissful spot
   Lost Eblis tempted man, she dared
To join the treach'rous angel's plot,
   And thus his crime and sentence shared
Her frightful claws remind her well
Of how she sinned and how she fell;
And when they meet her startled eyes,
Her fearful shrieks appal the skies!

The parrot talks and does his best
   To make life pass with cheerful mien,
In hopes that in the regions blest
Man will befriend and take him in.
The bat retires to some lone cell,
   Where worldly noise can ne'er intrude;
Where he in shade may calmly dwell,
   And spend the day in solitude.
Modest and peaceful, well he knows
   How frail is man, how false his ways;
And turns him from day's empty shows,
   And from the sun's intemperate blaze.

The Rose Garden of Persia

He is enamoured of the night,
  And while no rival comes between,
The stars can yield him ample light,
  When he may watch and gaze unseen;
Then he retires to muse once more,
On all her beauty's wondrous store;
And feels fair night has charms for him,
To which day's garish rays are dim.

The bee draws forth from fruit and flower
Sweet dews, that swell his golden dower;
But never injures by his kiss
Those who have made him rich in bliss.

The moth, though tortured by the flame,
Still hovers round and loves the same:
Nor is his fond attachment less—
  "Alas!" he whispers, "can it be,
Spite of my ceaseless tenderness,
  That I am doomed to death by thee?"

NIZAMI

Nizami, the first of the "romantic poets," flourished in the sixth year of the Hejira, and was surnamed Canjehur, from his native city in the province of Orran, near Berdaa.

His principal works are called the *Five Treasures*: they are, *The Loves of Khosrû and Shireen*; *The Loves of Mejnoun and Leila*; *The Sikander Namah* (Life of Alexander); *The Seven Beauties*; and a moral poem called *The Magazine of Mysteries*.

Nizami has succeeded beyond all other poets on the subject of Shireen, although he did not neglect any of the popular traditions of Persia. This is acknowledged as his *chef d'œuvre*.

THE STORY OF KHOSRÛ PARVIZ

Khosrû Parviz lived A.D. 590: he was a prince of exalted virtues and great magnificence: he fought against the Greek emperors with success, but was at last defeated by Heraclius. He is said to have married a daughter of the Emperor Maurice, named Irene, called by the Persians Shireen, or Sweet.

Ferhâd's history forms a tragical episode in this romance. He was a statuary, celebrated throughout the East for his great genius, but was daring enough to fix his affections on the beloved of a king. The jealousy of Khosrû was excited, and he lamented to his courtiers the existence of a passion which was so violent as not to be concealed, and which gave him great uneasiness. He was recommended to employ Ferhâd in such a manner as to occupy his whole life, and divert him from his dangerous dream: accordingly, as on one occasion the fair Shireen had, somewhat unreasonably, required of her royal lover a *river of milk*, he made her desire a pretext for the labours he imposed on his presumptuous rival.

Ferhâd was summoned to the presence of Khosrû, and commissioned by the king to

Nizami

execute a work which should render his name immortal, but one which, to accomplish, demanded almost superhuman powers: this was to clear away all impediments which obstructed the passage of the great mountain of Beysitoun, at that time impassable in consequence of its mighty masses of rock and stone. He commanded him, after having done this, to cause the rivers on the opposite side of the mountain to join.

Ferhâd, nothing daunted, replied that he would remove the very heart of the rock from the king's path; but on condition that the lovely Shireen should be the reward of his labours. Khosrû, secretly triumphing in the conviction that what the artist undertook was impossible, consented to his terms, and the indefatigable lover began his work.

THE LABOURS OF FERHÂD

On lofty Beysitoun the lingering sun
Looks down on ceaseless labours, long
    begun:

The Rose Garden of Persia

The mountain trembles to the echoing sound
Of falling rocks, that from her sides rebound.
Each day all respite, all repose denied—
No truce, no pause, the thundering strokes are plied;
The mist of night around her summit coils,
But still Ferhâd, the lover-artist, toils,
And still—the flashes of his axe between—
He sighs to ev'ry wind, "Alas! Shireen!
Alas! Shireen!—my task is well-nigh done,
The goal in view for which I strive alone.
Love grants me powers that Nature might deny;
 And, whatsoe'er my doom, the world shall tell,
Thy lover gave to immortality
 Her name he loved—so fatally—so well!"

 The enamoured sculptor prophesied aright; for the wonderful efforts made by this "slave

Nizami

of love" left imperishable monuments of his devotion, in the *carved caverns* which, to this day, excite the amazement and admiration of the traveller who visits the Kesr-e-Shireen, or "Villa of Shireen," and follows the stream called Joui-shur, or "stream of milk," which flows from the mountain, between Hamadân and Hulwân.

Ferhâd first constructed a recess or chamber in the rock, wherein he carved the figure of Shireen, near the front of the opening: she was represented surrounded by attendants and guards; while in the centre of the cave was an equestrian statue of Khosrû, clothed in armour, the workmanship so exquisite that the nails and buttons of the coat of mail were clearly to be seen, and are said to be so still. An eye-witness says: "Whoso looks on the stone would imagine it to be animated." The chamber and the statues remain still there. As Ferhâd continued to hew away pieces of the rock, which *are like as many columns*, the task was soon performed. The vestiges of the chisel remain, so that the sculptures appear recent. The horse of

The Rose Garden of Persia

Khosrû was exquisitely carved: it was called Shebdiz.

THE GREAT WORK

A hundred arms were weak one block to move
Of thousands, moulded by the hand of Love
Into fantastic shapes and forms of grace,
Which crowd each nook of that majestic place.

The piles give way, the rocky peaks divide,
The stream comes gushing on—a foaming tide!
A mighty work, for ages to remain,
The token of his passion and his pain.

As flows the milky flood from Allah's throne,
Rushes the torrent from the yielding stone;

Nizami

And sculptured there, amazed, stern Khosrû stands,
And sees, with frowns, obeyed his harsh commands:
While she, the fair beloved, with being rife,
Awakes the glowing marble into life.

Ah! hapless youth; ah! toil repaid by woe,—
A king thy rival and the world thy foe!
Will *she* wealth, splendour, pomp for thee resign?
And only genius, truth, and passion thine!

Around the pair, lo! groups of courtiers wait,
And slaves and pages crowd in solemn state;
From columns imaged wreaths their garlands throw,
And fretted roofs with stars appear to glow;

The Rose Garden of Persia

Fresh leaves and blossoms seem around to spring,
And feathered throngs their loves are murmuring;
The hands of Peris might have wrought those stems,
Where dewdrops hang their fragile diadems;
And strings of pearl and sharp-cut diamonds shine,
New from the wave, or recent from the mine.

"Alas! Shireen!" at every stroke he cries;
At every stroke fresh miracles arise:
"For thee these glories and these wonders all,
For thee I triumph, or for thee I fall;
For thee my life one ceaseless toil has been,
Inspire my soul anew: Alas! Shireen!"

The task of the rival of Khosrû was at length completed, and the king heard with dismay of his success: all the courtiers were

Nizami

terrified at the result of their advice, and saw that some further stratagem was necessary. They therefore engaged an old woman who had been known to Ferhâd, and in whom he had confidence, to report to him tidings which would at once destroy his hopes.

THE MESSENGER

What raven note disturbs his musing
    mood?
What form comes stealing on his solitude?
Ungentle messenger, whose word of ill
All the warm feelings of his soul can chill!

"Cease, idle youth, to waste thy days,"
    she said,
"By empty hopes a visionary made;
Why in vain toil thy fleeting life consume
To frame a palace?—rather hew a
    tomb.
Even like sere leaves that autumn winds
    have shed,
Perish thy labours, for—Shireen is dead!"

The Rose Garden of Persia

He heard the fatal news—no word, no
    groan;
He spoke not, moved not,—stood trans-
    fixed to stone.
Then, with a frenzied start, he raised on
    high
His arms, and wildly tossed them towards
    the sky;
Far in the wide expanse his axe he flung,
And from the precipice at once he sprung.
The rocks, the sculptured caves, the
    valleys green,
Sent back his dying cry—"Alas! Shireen!"

The legend goes on to relate that the handle of the axe flung away by Ferhâd, being of pomegranate wood, took root on the spot where it fell, and became a flourishing tree: it possessed healing powers, and was much resorted to by believers long afterwards.

Khosrû, on learning this catastrophe, did not conceal his satisfaction, but liberally rewarded the old woman who had caused so fatal a termination to the career of his rival;

Nizami

but the gentle-hearted Shireen heard of his fate with grief, and shed many tears on his tomb.

The charms of Shireen were destined to create mischief, for the king had a son by a former marriage, who became enamoured of his fatally beautiful mother-in-law. His father, Khosrû, was, in the end, murdered by his hand, and Shireen became the object of his importunities. Wearied, at length, with constant struggles, she feigned to give him a favourable answer, and promised, if he would permit her to visit the grave of her husband, *when she returned* she would be his. Shireen accordingly went on her melancholy errand, and, true to her affection for her beloved Khosrû, stabbed herself, and died upon his tomb.

SADI

THE great poet Sadi is esteemed amongst the Persians as a master in poetry and in morality. He is better known in Europe than any other Eastern author except Hafiz, and has been more frequently translated. Jami calls him "The Nightingale of the Groves of Shiráz," of which city (which can boast of being the birthplace of some of the most celebrated men of Persia) he was a native.

Sadi was born about 1194, and his life extended, it is said, over a period of one hundred and two years, great part of which time he spent in travel and the acquisition of knowledge, and a considerable portion in retirement and devotion. He is called "the most poignant of the eloquent," and his works are termed "the salt-mine of poets," being revered as unrivalled models of the first genius in the world.

Sadi

His descent was good, though his family was decayed in point of wealth, and some of its members were engaged in commercial pursuits. Though he was twice married during his long career, like our own great poet Milton, his opinion of women is by no means flattering, as, for instance, when he says—

"Take your wife's opinion, and act in opposition to it."

On another occasion he most ungallantly observes—

"Choose a fresh wife every spring, or new year's day; for the almanac of last year is good for nothing."

His philosophy enabled him to support all the ills of life with patience and fortitude; and one of his remarks, arising from the destitute condition in which he once found himself, is deserving preservation—

"I never complained of my condition but once, *when my feet were bare, and I had not money to buy shoes:* but I met a man *without feet*, and became contented with my lot."

When a boy he confesses to have been religious overmuch, and mentions a judicious reproof of his father, on his ridiculing some friends who fell asleep while the Koran was being read. "You had better," said he, "have been asleep yourself than occupied in discovering faults in your neighbours."

Sadi made the holy pilgrimage no less than fourteen times; and so great was his reputation for sanctity, that his admirers look upon him as a saint, and attribute to him the power of working miracles. He led the life for some time of a *sacayi*, or water-drawer, in the Holy Land, and was accustomed to administer to the wants of the thirsty traveller, till at length he was found worthy of an introduction to the prophet Khizr — a mysterious personage, the subject of endless allusion in Eastern works,—who moistened his mouth with the waters of immortality. To doubt this legend was considered sacrilegious. Several other poets, it seems, applied for a draught to this keeper of "the sacred well," but without success. Hafiz, however, boasts, and his followers believe, that he obtained some of its inspiring waters.

Sadi

The works of Sadi are very numerous, and all popular and familiar in every mouth in the East. His two greatest works are the *Bostān* and *Gulistān*, which abound in striking beauties, and show great purity of feeling and knowledge of human nature.

CONTENTMENT

FROM THE BOSTĀN

Smile not, nor think the legend vain,
   That in old times a worthless stone
Such power in holy hands could gain,
   That straight a silver heap it shone.
Thy alchemist Contentment be,
Equal is stone or ore to thee.

The infant's pure unruffled breast
No avarice nor pride molest:
He fills his little hands with earth,
Nor knows that silver has more worth.

The sultan sits in pomp and state,
And sees the dervish at his gate;

The Rose Garden of Persia

But yet of wealth the sage has more
Than the great king, with all his store.

Rich is a beggar, worn and spent,
   To whom a silver coin is thrown;
But Feridoun was not content,
   Though Ajum's kingdom was his own.

Most of the prose works of Sadi are mixed with verse, a custom very general with Oriental writers. In every department of poetry he excelled, and all he touched was rendered valuable. The favourite romances of Persia were not left unnoticed by him, but these subjects are generally thought to have been more successfully treated by Nizami, Hatifi, and Jami.

A variety of romantic anecdotes are told of Sadi in his travels: the following is singularly wild and poetical:—

"Sadi, when in Armenia, became much attached to a young man of his own age. In that country people died not the natural death, but on a particular day, once a year, they were in the habit of meeting on a plain

Sadi

near their principal cities, when they occupied themselves in recreation and amusement, in the midst of which individuals of every age and rank would suddenly stop, make a reverence to the west, gird up their loins, and, setting out full speed towards that quarter of the desert, were no more seen or heard of.

"Sadi had often remarked that the relations of those persons made few observations or explanations on their disappearance. At last, on such an anniversary, Sadi observed that his friend was preparing to set off, when he seized upon his girdle, and insisted upon knowing what it meant. The youth solemnly enjoined him to let him go, for that the Malic-al-mo-at, or angel of death, had already called on him twice, and on the third call he must obey his destiny, whether he would or no; but Sadi kept his hold, and found himself carried along with such velocity as deprived him of the power of knowing whither they went. At last they stopped in a verdant plain in the midst of the desert, when the youth stretched himself upon the earth: the turf opened, and he was swallowed up.

The Rose Garden of Persia

"Sadi threw dust over the spot, lamented him in beautiful verse, and set about finding the way back: he had to cross rivers of molten gold, silver, and copper, through deserts and wildernesses, and over mountains of snow, before he found himself once more at the place from whence he had started."

ON TRUE WORTH

Although a gem be cast away,
And lie obscured in heaps of clay,
  Its precious worth is still the same:
Although vile dust be whirled to heaven,
To such no dignity is given,
  Still base as when from earth it came.

I saw the demon in a dream,
  But how unlike he seemed to be,
To all of horrible we deem,
  And all of fearful that we see.
His shape was like a cypress bough,
  His eyes like those that Houris wear,
His face as beautiful as though
  The rays of Paradise were there.

Sadi

I near him came, and spoke—"Art
 thou,"
 I said, "indeed the Evil One?
No angel has so bright a brow,
 Such yet no eye has looked upon.
Why should mankind make *thee* a jest,
 When thou canst show a face like
 this?
Fair as the moon in splendour drest,
 An eye of joy, a smile of bliss!
The painter draws thee vile to sight,
 Our baths thy frightful form display;
They told me thou wert black as night,
 Behold! thou art as fair as day!"
The lovely vision's ire awoke,
 His voice was loud, and proud his
 mien,—
"Believe not, friend," 'twas thus he
 spoke,
 "That thou my likeness yet hast seen:
The pencil that my portrait made
 Was guided by an envious foe;
In Paradise I man betrayed,
 And he, from hatred, paints me so."

ATTAR

Ferid-ed-deen Attar, of Nizapoor, was called the "scourge of spiritual men"; he was one of the great Sufi masters, and his life was spent in devotion and contemplation. He lived in the reign of Sanjah, in A.D. 1119, and, in common with several other famous poets, died at a very advanced age, namely, that of 114 years. It would seem that poetry in the East was favourable to human life, by so many of its professors attaining to such an age, particularly those who professed the Sufi doctrine.

His great work is the *Perid Namah*, a moral poem, containing useful maxims, of which the following are specimens:—

THE WAY TO PARADISE

Wouldst thou inherit Paradise,
These maxims keep before thine eyes;

Attar

So thy heart's mirror shall appear,
For ever shining bright and clear.
Give thanks when Fortune smiles serene,
Be patient when her frown is seen;
If thou hast sinned, for pardon plead,
And help shall follow at thy need.
But shall he hope the prize to hold,
Who with new sins conceals the old?
Be penitent, be watchful still,
And fly the votaries of ill;
Avoid the paths that lead to vice,
And win thy way to Paradise.

THE PRAISE OF THE ALMIGHTY

Unbounded praise to God be given,
Who from His throne, the height of heaven,
Looked on this handful of frail earth—
Unnoticed man—and gave him birth.

On Adam breathed, and bade the wave
Pause, and His servant, Noah, save;
The tempest, with His terrors clad,
And swept from earth the tribe of Ad.

The Rose Garden of Persia

And for His "friend," O blissful name
To roses changed a bed of flame:
The smallest insect at His will,
Becomes an instrument of ill.

He spoke, the sea o'erwhelms His foes,
And the hard rock a camel grows!
The iron turns, at His command,
To pliant wax, in David's hand.

To Solomon, He gave his sway,
And bade the Dives his sign obey;
To one a diadem is given,
Another's head the *saw* has riven.

Impartial in His goodness still,
Equal to all is good or ill.

One lies on Persian silk reclined,
One naked in a frozen wind;
One scarce can count his heaps of ore;
One faints with hunger at the door.

He bade a virgin's child appear,
And made an infant's witness clear.

Attar

The Dives before His vengeance fly,
By hosts of stars expelled the sky,
And kings, who hold the world in thrall,
At His great word to ruin fall.

THE MOOLAH OF RÛM

JELAL-ED-DIN RÛMI, usually called *The Moolah*, was born at Balkh, a city of Khorassan. His father, Boha-ed-din Veled, enjoyed distinguished honours there, under the domination of Shah Mohammed Kharizm. He was an enthusiastic follower of the doctrine of the Sufis, and became so celebrated as a preacher and expounder, that people flocked from all parts of Persia to hear him discourse. He died in the year of the Hejira 631 (A.D. 1233).

His son succeeded him as head of the sect, but surpassed his father, not only in the peculiar virtues and attainments of the Sufis, but by his splendid poetical genius. Retired from the world, wholly absorbed in meditation, and in a total forgetfulness of his material existence, he never appeared to men except to reveal the august secrets of

The Moolah of Rûm

his mysterious doctrine, and living the most perfect model of a Sufi, this "precious pearl of the ocean of mysticism quitted this fragile world" in A.D. 1272, at the age of sixty-nine years.

His famous poems are collected into a book called *Kullyat-al Mesnevy*. They are generally regarded as the most perfect models of the mystic style; but its obscurity is a great obstacle to the thorough comprehension of the compositions. "There is," says Sir William Jones, "a depth and solemnity in his works unequalled by any poet of this class; even Hafiz must be considered inferior to him."

A Persian critic was asked how it happened that the two most celebrated Persian Sufi poets should differ so much in their description of love.

Hafiz observes: "Love, at first sight, appeared easy, but afterwards full of difficulties."

The Moolah, in direct opposition, says: "Love at first resembles a murderer, that he may alarm all who are without his pale."

The Rose Garden of Persia

"Poor Hafiz," says the critic, "did not find out till the last what the wiser Moolah saw at a glance."

The following is a specimen of his lighter poetry:—

THE FAIREST LAND

"Tell me, gentle traveller, thou
  Who hast wandered far and wide,
Seen the sweetest roses blow,
  And the brightest rivers glide;
Say, of all thine eyes have seen,
Which the fairest land has been?"

"Lady, shall I tell thee where
Nature seems most blest and fair,
Far above all climes beside?—
'Tis where those we love abide:
And that little spot is best
Which the loved one's foot hath pressed.

"Though it be a fairy space,
Wide and spreading is the place;

The Moolah of Rûm

Though 'twere but a barren mound,
'Twould become enchanted ground.

"With thee yon sandy waste would seem
The margin of Al Cawthar's stream;
And thou canst make a dungeon's gloom
A bower where new-born roses bloom."

HAFIZ

AMONGST all the poets of Persia, he whose *name*, if not his works, is most familiar to the English reader is Mohammed Schems-ed-din Hafiz, the prince of Persian lyric poets, of whom Shiràz may boast, that to that charming city a greater charm was added in his birth, at the beginning of the fourteenth century of the Christian era. His surname of Hafiz indicates that he was master of the whole Koran, the word expressing *keeper*, or *possessor*. Leading a life of poverty, of which he was proud,—for he considered poverty the companion of genius,—he constantly refused the invitations of monarchs to visit their courts; and only once yielded to these frequent solicitations in the instance of the Prince of Yezd, whose want of generosity confirmed him in his resolution never again to leave his native place, where

Hafiz

he remained till his death, in the year of the Hejira 791 (A.D. 1389).

The endless variety of the poems of Hafiz, their brilliancy, energy, and originality, are so striking, that, as Sir William Jones justly remarks, it is difficult to select specimens, so replete with surpassing beauty, thought, feeling, and expression are they. To open his book at hazard, and fix on the first lines that occur, is a safe plan, as it is impossible to choose amiss in that garden of ever-blooming roses.

The grace, ease, and fancy of his numbers are inimitable, like those of our own poet Moore; and there is a Magic in his lays which few, even of his professed enemies, have been able to resist. To the young, the gay, and the enthusiastic, his verses are ever welcome, and the sage discovers in them a hidden mystery, which reconciles him to their subjects.

There is a curious story told of the dispute which occurred at the time of his death, between those who condemned and those who admired the poet. The former objected

The Rose Garden of Persia

to his being buried in consecrated ground; the latter insisted that he had never offended against religion or morals, and deserved every honour that could be bestowed. It was at length agreed that a line of his own should decide, and, the book being opened at the following passage, all opposition was overcome at once:—

"Withdraw not your steps from the obsequies of Hafiz; though immersed in sin, he will rise in Paradise."

His tomb, near Shirâz, has been, from that day, visited as a sacred spot by pilgrims of all ages: the place of his birth is held in veneration, and there is not a Persian whose heart does not echo his strains; and is there a poet's in England which does not respond to the exquisite translation, by Sir William Jones, of those beautiful mysterious verses beginning, "Sweet maid, if thou wouldst charm my sight"?

Hafiz has been called the Persian Anacreon: in this character he composed the following Kasidah and Gazels, to which Sir William Jones alone could do justice:—

Hafiz

THE FEAST OF SPRING

My breast is filled with roses,
  My cup is crowned with wine,
And by my side reposes
  The maid I hail as mine.
The monarch, wheresoe'er he be,
Is but a slave compared to me!

Their glare no torches throwing
  Shall in our bower be found;
Her eyes, like moonbeams glowing,
  Cast light enough around:
And well all odours I can spare,
Who scent the perfume of her hair.

The honey-dew thy charm might borrow,
  Thy lip alone to me is sweet;
When thou art absent, faint with sorrow
  I hide me in some lone retreat.
Why talk to me of power or fame?—
  What are those idle toys to me?
Why ask the praises of my name?
  My joy, my triumph is in thee!

The Rose Garden of Persia

How blest am I! around me, swelling,
    The notes of melody arise;
I hold the cup, with juice excelling,
    And gaze upon thy radiant eyes.
O Hafiz!—never waste thy hours
    Without the cup, the lute, and love!
For 'tis the sweetest time of flowers,
    And none these moments shall reprove
The nightingales around thee sing,
It is the joyous feast of spring.

THE SEASON OF THE ROSE

String the lyre!—Has Fortune ever
    Given to men of worth their due?
Then, since vain is all endeavour,
    And we scorn her malice too,
Why should we refuse to share
All the joys these hours prepare?
Now the air is filled with mirth;
Now the roses spring from earth;
Now they bloom, but now alone,—
    Fear not, though the wise reprove;
Ere their soft perfume be gone,
    Raise the soul to verse and love.

Hafiz

O Hafiz!—it were shame to say,
  —In nightingales like us 'twere treason,—
That we, who make the magic lay,
  Sang not in the rose's season.

THE OMEN

This morning I resolved, at last,
All idle thoughts far hence to cast,
And in repentance steep my soul,—
Forgot the roses and the bowl!
"Oh, let some omen be my guide,
And I will follow it," I cried:
But say, alas! what could I do?
  'Twas spring, that breaker of all vows;—
I saw the trees their leaves renew,
  I saw fresh roses on the boughs:
I saw the merry cup go round,
My rivals with enjoyment crowned!
Whilst I, a looker-on, must see
All gay and full of hope but me!

The Rose Garden of Persia

One draught!—but one!—that drunk, I fly
At once this dang'rous company.
But ah!—*she* came!—as buds to light,
My heart expanded at her sight,
And every strong resolve gave way—
My rivals saw me blest as they!
I'll seat my love amidst the bower,
   With rosy garlands bind her hair;
Wreathe round her arms the jasmine flower,
   Than those white chains more sweet and fair,
Away!—I was not born a sage;
Am I the censor of the age?—
Is mine a priest's or judge's part,
   To chide at mirth and love like this?
Elated, like the rose, my heart
   Throws off its shrouding veil for bliss.
Why should I censure wine? fill full
To her, the kind, the beautiful.
If but one kiss I should obtain,
Youth and delight were mine again;
And I another age should live,
Such power the smiles of beauty give.

Hafiz

Reproach me, then, ye wise, no more,
  Nor say I joy in *secret* pleasure;
Let all behold my cup run o'er,
  While harp and lute keep joyous measure.

ON HIS TRAVELS

The world to me has been a home;
  Wherever knowledge could be sought,
Through differing climes I loved to roam,
  And every shade of feeling caught
From minds, whose varied fruits supply
The food of my philosophy.
And still the treasures of my store
  Have made my wanderings less severe;
From every spot some prize I bore,
  From every harvest gleaned an ear,
But find no land can ever vie
With bright Shiráz in purity;
And blest for ever be the spot
Which makes all other climes forgot!

The Rose Garden of Persia

GAZEL ON HIS LOVE

Sweet breeze! her breath thy murmurs bear,
  The perfume of her sigh is thine;
But dare not play amidst her hair,
  For every golden curl is mine!
O rose! what radiant hues hast thou,
That in her face less brightly glow!
Her love is joy without regret,
While briars and thorns thy bloom beset.

O opening buds!—her cheeks more fair,
For ever rosy blushing are.
Narcissus!—thou art pale of hue,
Her eyes that languish, sparkle too;
I tell thee, gently waving pine!
More graceful is her form than thine.

O my rapt soul! if thou hadst power
To choose all blessings earth can give,
Is there a better, richer dower
Than for her tenderness to live?

Hafiz

Come, my sole love! from those dear eyes
  Thy Hafiz is too long away;
Come, give his heart the sweet surprise,
  Though 'twere but for a single day!

MYSTIC ODE

In wide Eternity's vast space,
  Where no beginning was, wert Thou:
The rays of all-pervading grace
  Beneath Thy veil flamed on Thy brow.
Then Love and Nature sprang to birth,
And Life and Beauty filled the earth.

Awake, my soul! pour forth thy praise
To that great Being anthems raise—
That wondrous Architect, who said,
"Be formed," and this great orb was made.

Since first I heard the blissful sound—
  "To man My Spirit's breath is given";
I knew, with thankfulness profound,
  His sons we are—our Home is heaven.

The Rose Garden of Persia

Oh! give me tidings that shall tell
When I may hope with Thee to dwell,
That I may quit this world of pain,
Nor seek to be its guest again.

A bird of holiness am I,
That from the vain world's net would fly;
Shed, bounteous Lord, one cheering shower
From Thy pure cloud of guiding power,
Before, even yet, the hour is come,
When my dust rises towards its home.

What are our deeds?—all worthless, all—
   Oh, bring Devotion's wine,
That strength upon my soul may fall
   From drops Thou mad'st divine.
The world's possessions fade and flee,
The only good is—loving Thee!

O happy hour! when I shall rise
From earth's delusions to the skies,
Shall find my soul at rest, and greet
The traces of my loved one's feet:
Dancing with joy, whirled on with speed,
Like motes that gorgeous sunbeams feed,

Hafiz

Until I reach the fountain bright
Whence yonder sun derives his light.

The reputation of Hafiz has not suffered from time, and he is still held in as much esteem as Shakespeare with us. In an amusing satire on the customs and manners of the women of Persia, called *Kitabi Kulsûm Naneh*, which in its style is not unlike the Sirventes of the Troubadours, are the following passages illustrative of the delight taken in the poet's verses:—

"The women of Shirâz have remarkable taste in minstrelsy, and are devoted to the memory of Hafiz.

"Every woman should be instructed in the art of playing on the *dyra*, or tambourine; and she in turn must teach it to her daughters, that their time may be passed in joy and mirth; and the songs of Hafiz, above all others, must be remembered. If it so happen that neither a *dyra nulkadâr* nor a *sikdâr* is in the house, at any rate there should be a *brass dish* and a *mallet* for the purpose of producing music."

The Rose Garden of Persia

The opinion of the learned Reviczki, given by Sir William Jones, that Hafiz was an *esprit fort*, and ridiculed the Koran and the Prophets, is not generally entertained in Persia, and his book is consulted in the same manner as Virgil has often been. Nadir Shah resolved on two famous sieges in consequence of two verses which he found on opening the volume of the poet's verses.

The famous Gazel of Hafiz, sung by every nautch-girl throughout India, is *Mutriba Khush* :—

"Mutriba Khush, his sweetest song."

The most familiar lines are "Taza be taza no be no," and the song is a peculiar favourite with the English, being set to one of the few pretty Eastern airs.

The beautiful poem of "Sweet maid, if thou wouldst charm my sight," of Sir William Jones, which begins—

"Egher ân turki Shiràzi,"

is considered a model of beautiful composition.

Hafiz

A PERSIAN SONG OF HAFIZ

Sweet maid, if thou wouldst charm my sight,
And bid these arms thy neck infold;
That rosy cheek, that lily hand,
Would give thy poet more delight
Than all Bocara's vaunted gold,
Than all the gems of Samarcand.

Boy, let yon liquid ruby flow,
And bid thy pensive heart be glad,
Whate'er the frowning zealots say:
Tell them, their Eden cannot show
A stream so clear as Rocnabad,
A bow'r so sweet as Mosellay.

Oh! when these fair perfidious maids,
Whose eyes our secret haunts infest,
Their dear destructive charms display,
Each glance my tender heart invades,
And robs my wounded soul of rest,
As Tartars seize their destined prey.

The Rose Garden of Persia

In vain with love our bosoms glow:
Can all our tears, can all our sighs,
New lustre to those charms impart?
Can cheeks, where living roses blow,
Where Nature spreads her richest dyes,
Require the borrowed gloss of art?

Speak not of fate:—ah! change the theme,
And talk of odours, talk of wine,
Talk of the flow'rs that round us bloom:
'Tis all a cloud, 'tis all a dream;
To love and joy thy thoughts confine,
Nor hope to pierce the sacred gloom.

Beauty has such resistless pow'r,
That ev'n the chaste Egyptian dame
Sighed for the blooming Hebrew boy:
For her how fatal was the hour
When to the banks of Nilus came
A youth so lovely and so coy!

But ah! sweet maid, my counsel hear
(Youth should attend when those advise
Whom long experience renders sage):
While music charms the ravished ear,

Hafiz

While sparkling cups delight our eyes,
Be gay, and scorn the frowns of age.

What cruel answer have I heard?
And yet, by Heav'n, I love thee still:
Can aught be cruel from thy lips?
Yet say, how fell that bitter word
From lips which streams of sweetness fill,
Which nought but drops of honey sip?

Go boldly forth, my simple lay,
Whose accents flow with artless ease,
Like orient pearls at random strung;
Thy notes are sweet, the damsels say,
But oh! far sweeter, if they please
The Nymph for whom these notes are sung.

The magic power possessed by Hafiz over his readers is easily accounted for, if the legend of his having quaffed of the mysterious cup of immortality be believed. The story, which is very poetical, runs thus:—

About four leagues from the city of Shiráz

The Rose Garden of Persia

is a place called Peri-sebz, or the "Green old Man," and a popular superstition prevailed that whoever watched there forty nights without sleep would become a great poet. Hafiz, when a youth, resolved to try the adventure: he was at this time in love with a beautiful "fair one," whose name of Shakhi Nebât expressed "a branch of sugar-cane," but he had a powerful rival in the Prince of Shirâz. Like Ferhâd, the lover of Shireen, he however was not to be daunted by the rank of him who pretended to the smiles of his charming favourite. Every morning he walked before the house of his coy mistress, anxiously watching for some sign of recognition which might give him hope; at noon he rested, and at night repaired to the place of the "green old man," and there took up his watchful station.

This he continued for thirty-nine nights, and on the fortieth morning was charmed to observe that his mistress beckoned to him from the balcony, and invited him to enter. She received him with enthusiasm, declaring

Hafiz

her preference of a bright genius to the son of a king. On the approach of night he hurried away, bent on finishing the adventure. Early on the morning, after his agitated fortieth night, the young poet perceived an aged man approaching. He could not see from whence he came, and could scarcely define his figure, which was wrapt in a green mantle; in his hand he bore a cup containing a crystal liquor, which sparkled and foamed as if it would overleap its narrow bounds. The aged man held out the vase to Hafiz, who, seizing it with avidity, drank an inspiring draught, and found in it the gift of immortal poesy.

JAMI

The favourite subject of the Loves of Yussuf and Zuleika, which every Persian poet has touched with more or less success, has never found one who so thoroughly entered into it, and rendered it so beautiful, as Jami. He entirely remodelled the poem of Ferdusi, and gave it so many new graces that his composition completely superseded that of his master, and his name is always peculiarly associated with those of the lovers whose "well-sung woes" he has so eloquently sung.

Jami was born in Khorassan, at the village of Jam, from whence he is named, his proper appellation being Abd' Arahman.

He was a Sufi, and preferred, like many of his fellow-poets, the meditations and ecstasies of mysticism to the pleasures of a court. He became, however, a friend of princes.

One of the great aims of the philosophic

and benevolent Jami was to instruct and improve his auditors; and in order to do so effectually, particularly as regarded the common people, he was accustomed to come frequently to the great mosque of Hérât, and there converse familiarly with all whom he met.

His eloquence was great, his manner persuasive, and his doctrine pure; and, like St. Aldelm, the friend of King Athelstan, he succeeded in attracting and riveting the attention of his hearers.

Jami died in 1492, mourned by the whole city of Hérât: his funeral expenses were defrayed by Sultan Hossein, and a magnificent train of the most illustrious nobles accompanied his body to the tomb; "and when the customary rites had been performed," say the Persians, "the earth, opening like a shell, received into its bosom this pearl of inestimable price." His funeral oration was composed by his friend Ali-Chyr, and delivered by a celebrated orator, twenty days after his interment, in the presence of the sultan, the sheikhs, the

The Rose Garden of Persia

doctors, and an immense concourse of people. Ali-Chyr laid the first stone of a monument which he caused to be raised to his memory, and his fame became immortal in the minds of his countrymen.

His writings are very voluminous; at Oxford twenty-two volumes are preserved of his works, of which he composed nearly forty, all of great length. The greater part treat of the theology of the Mussulmans, or are written in the mystic style. He collected the most interesting under the name of *Haft-Aurenk,* or "The Seven Stars of the Bear, or the Seven Brothers"; and amongst these is the famous poem of Yussuf and Zuleika.

The tale extends in the original to four thousand couplets. Sir William Jones pronounces it to be "the *finest* poem he ever read"; and nothing can exceed the admiration which it inspires in the East. The abridged version which is here offered may, perhaps, convey some notion of its style, though I offer rather an adaptation than a translation.

The name of the wife of Potiphar is not

Jami

mentioned in the Koran, but the poets have given her the appellation of Zuleika, though she is by some Arabian commentators called Rahil. Her history, as given by her poetical biographers, presents a very different picture from that which we have been accustomed to look on. Her love, disappointment, weakness, despair, and final happiness, form the features of a most exciting drama, and one the most remarkable in Oriental literature.

Zuleika, the daughter of Taimus, king of Mauritania, beheld in a dream a figure of such extraordinary beauty that she became immediately enamoured of the glorious vision, and sunk into a deep melancholy, fruitlessly longing for the unknown object. This dream was three times repeated, and the last time the beautiful apparition named Egypt as the land of his abode. The state of Zuleika's mind is thus described:—

The ravens of the night were hushed,
  The bird of dawn began his lay,
The rosebud, newly awakened, blushed
  To feel the touch of springing day,

The Rose Garden of Persia

And bade the roses round unveil,
Roused by the warbling nightingale.
The jasmine stood all bathed in dew;
Wet were the violet's lids of blue.

Zuleika, fairer than the flowers,
　Lay tranced—for 'twas not sleep that stole
Her senses, through the night's still hours,
　And raised new visions to her soul.
The heart unfettered, free to rove,
Turned towards the idol of her love.

No:—'twas not sleep, 'twas motionless,
　Unbroken thought, repressed in vain;
The shadow of the day's distress,
　A frenzy of remembered pain.

But, 'midst those pangs, what rapture still!
　The same dear form is ever there;
Those eyes the rays of Eden fill,
And odours of the blest distil
　From every curl of that bright hair!

Jami

His smiles!—such smiles as Houris wear,
  When from their caves of pearl they come,
And bid the true believer share
  The pleasures of their sacred home.

See, on his shoulder shines a star
  That glows and dazzles as he moves:
She feels its influence afar,
  She gazes, worships, hopes—and loves!

At this period, while her mind is absorbed by the one engrossing idea, an embassy arrives in Mauritania from that very country, Egypt, the land of all her hopes, soliciting the hand of the princess for the Asis, or grand vizir of Pharaoh, an offer which she unhesitatingly accepts, being secretly convinced that her visionary lover and her proposed future husband are the same. She accordingly departs for Egypt, with a splendid and numerous retinue, and makes a magnificent entry into Memphis, under the escort of the Asis Potiphar, or Kitfîr, himself, who comes to meet his bride. Curious to discover his identity, she anxiously seizes an opportunity of peeping through the curtains of her litter, but is filled with grief and dismay on finding a totally different person from the lovely image of her dreams.

She thus exclaims, on hearing the acclamations which announce the arrival of the Asis, when he first comes to meet her, before she has yet made the discovery fatal to her peace :—

O joy too great !—O hour too blest !
  He comes—they hail him—now, more near,
  His eager courser's feet I hear.
O heart ! be hushed within my breast,
Burst not with rapture ! Can it be?
  The idol of my life—divine,
All radiant, clothed in mystery,
  And loving me as I adore,
  As none dared ever love before,
Shall be—nay, *is*—even now, is mine !

I will be patient, but his breath
Seems stealing o'er my senses—death

Jami

Were better than suspense like this—
One draught—though 'twere the last—of
    bliss!
One glance, though in that glance I die,
To prove the glorious certainty!

Her horror and despair on finding how much her fancy had deluded her knew no bounds:—

Not he! not he! on whom for years
    My soul has dwelt with sacred truth;
For whom my life has passed in tears,
    And wasted was my bloom of youth;
For whom I breathed, and thought, and
    moved,
My own, my worshipped, my beloved!

I hailed the night, that I might gaze
Upon his star's unconquered blaze:
The morn but rose that I might pray,
Hope, wish, expect from day to day,
My sole existence was that thought,
And do I wake to know 'tis nought?
Vain tears, vain madness, vain endeavour,
Another blasts my sight for ever!

The Rose Garden of Persia

In the meantime the unconscious bridegroom, exulting in his happiness, conducts the gorgeous train of attendants, with a great display of pomp and riches, to usher his bride of far-famed beauty into the city of Memphis.

ZULEIKA'S ENTRANCE INTO MEMPHIS

Dawn upon the wide world broke,
And the sun's warm rays awoke;
Scattering o'er the cloudy sky
Hues of rich variety:
Such bright tinting as illumes
With its rays the peacock's plumes,
And the parrot's feathers bright
Touches with a starry light.
The Asis rides in kingly guise;
Yon curtained litter holds the prize
More precious than all wealth beside—
His own, his young, his peerless bride.

Around, afar, of homage proud,
In countless ranks his warriors crowd;

Jami

Well may the lordly Asis boast
The glories of his gorgeous host.
Rich are the veils, profusely spread,
That canopy the "fair one's" head;
Like some delicious tree that throws
Its shade, inviting to repose:
And, like soft turf, the carpets lie,
Bedecked with gay embroidery.

The temple moves, all-glorious, on—
Throned in the midst the "happy one."
All heaven resounds with shout and song,
As the bright pageant sweeps along.
The camel-drivers' cries succeed,
Urging their stately beasts to speed,
Whose hoofs, with swift and frequent tread,
The sands with moonlike forms have spread;
The earth is ploughed by coursers' feet,
And still fresh hosts the wounds repeat.
Many a fair and blushing maid
Exulted in the gay parade:
And all who called the Asis lord
Hailed the fair idol he adored.

The Rose Garden of Persia

But she—"the beautiful," "the blest,"—
What pangs, what tumults shook her breast!
She sat, concealed from every eye,—
Alone—in hopeless misery.
"O Fate!" she cried; "O ruthless Fate!
Why am I made thy mark of hate?
Why must my heart thy victim be?
Thus lost, abandoned—crushed by thee!
Thou camest, in troubled dreams, and stole
The peace, the pleasure of my soul,
In visions that the blest might share,
Whose only fruit has been despair.
I see each glittering fabric fall;
But vain reproach, vain trust, vain all!
For help, for rest, where can I fly?
My heart is riven—let me die!

Have I then lingered long in pain,
In sad suspense, in musings vain,
To be—O crowning grief! betrayed,
In foreign lands a victim made?
Relentless destiny! accurst
Were all the joys thy visions nurst.

Jami

Is there no drop of hope left yet?
Must I *all* promises forget?
Dash not my cup to earth: say, Power benign,
I may be blest—even yet he may be mine!"

In a similar strain to these upbraidings of "the fair one" is Timon's indignant address to the Deity who persecutes him, as Lucian records it.

"He besieges Jupiter with a storm of epithets, and railing at the dotage into which the god has fallen, and his imbecility in permitting so much evil in the world. He reminds him of the former times, in which his lightning and thunders were in constant occupation, etc. etc. He then comes to his own particular case, and upbraids the god for allowing him to be treated with so much ingratitude."

"Why," continues Zuleika distractedly, "hast thou thus cruelly robbed me of my peace? What have I done to thee to be thus treated; it is folly indeed that I seek

The Rose Garden of Persia

help from thee. When souls melt, thou art
called upon for aid; what is the melting of
thy soul?"

Thus raved Zuleika, when without
Arose the sudden deafening shout
That hailed the close of all their toil—
"Lo!—Memphis! and the banks of
    Nile!"

Then, far and wide, the glittering ranks
Rush to the flowery river's banks.
The Asis' sign his slaves obey,
Gold, silver, flowers, bestrew the way!
And o'er the litter gems are thrown,
Whose countless rays like meteors shone;
As thick they fall as on the rose
Hang the rich dews at evening's close;
The courser's feet on rubies trod,
O'er mounds of gold the camel strode.

On swept the train—one gorgeous mile,
Planting with gems the banks of Nile;
The proud stream rolled its waters deep
O'er pearls in many a shining heap:

Jami

Each shell was filled with pearls; each scale
That clothed the crocodile in mail
Was changed to silver, as he lay
And basked amidst the fervid ray.

The original is slightly altered in the above; it runs in this curious strain:—

"Thus, *for a whole mile*, the procession moved on, scattering jewels on the banks of the Nile; the proud stream was filled with imperial pearls; *every fish's ear was a pearl shell*, and so much silver was thrown in that the crocodile became a *silver-scaled fish*."

And onward to the palace gate
The train poured on, in sumptuous state;
The glowing portals opened wide,—
In flowed the overwhelming tide,
Ushering the Asis and his bride.

A throne the Peris might have framed,
The sun and moon's pale lustre shamed:

The Rose Garden of Persia

And she, whose radiance all effaced—
Zuleika—on the throne was placed.
Sparkling with jewels, red with gold,
Her heart shrunk, withered, crushed, and
 cold;

Although a feverish sense of pain
Frenzied her mind and seared her
 brain:
As on a flaming hearth she sat—
Amidst rejoicing—desolate!
Laden with many a priceless gem,
Crowned with a gorgeous diadem,
Each pearl a poisonous drop appears:
And from her eyes fall scalding tears.

And thus a crown is gained—for this,
We leave all thoughts of present bliss!
We toil, we strive, we live in care,
And in the end possess—despair!
Our sun of youth, of hope, is set,
And all our guerdon is—regret!

This profusion at the marriage of persons
of consequence is by no means unusual in the

East. It is related that Mahadie, the son of El Mansor, the founder of Bagdad, in his pilgrimages, expended enormous sums; in one alone he is said to have disbursed six million dinars of gold. He founded cisterns and caravanseras, and distributed them along a measured road of seven hundred miles. His train of camels, *laden with snow*, was prodigious; this was a luxury intended to refresh the fruits and liquors of the royal banquet. He gave away four-fifths of the income of a province before he drew his foot from the stirrup. At his nuptials a thousand pearls of the largest size were showered on the head of the bride, and a lottery was made of lands and houses.

The poem now pursues the scriptural account of the life of Yussuf, whose supernatural beauty is, however, described as being the especial gift of God, and recorded to have been so great, that no woman could look on him without love. Zuleika, therefore, only shared the fate of all her sex. Some writers say the ladies who clamoured so much against her for her passion were, when he first entered the chamber where they were all assembled, in the act of cutting pomegranates, some say oranges, and in their admiration and amazement cut their fingers instead of the fruit. This adventure is frequently represented in Persian MSS. —see several in the British Museum, and Bib. du Roi, Paris. Joseph is considered the emblem of divine perfection, and Zuleika's love is the image of the love of the creature towards the Creator: some go so far as to say that we ought to follow her example, and should permit the beauty of God to transport us out of ourselves. The rapid change from prison to high estate of Yussuf (or Joseph) they consider a type of the impatience of the soul to burst its fetters and join its Creator. His great charity is constantly spoken of. Sâdi praises him for this in his *Gulistân*, and relates that during the seven years' famine in Egypt, Yussuf deprived himself, every day, of a portion of his food, to give to the sufferers: this trait is often mentioned by Eastern writers.

Yussuf was always surrounded with a

Jami

celestial light, typical of the moral beauty and wisdom which adorned his mind.

He is sold as a slave, and Zuleika becomes his purchaser, to the great rage and envy of all her rivals, amongst whom was included the Princess Nasigha, of the race of Aad. The beautiful Yussuf now enters her service, and, at his own desire, a flock of sheep are given to his special keeping, his admiring mistress wishing, by every indulgence, to attach him to her.

The nurse of Zuleika is the confidante of the passion which she cannot control, and which, at length, in an imprudent moment, she discloses to its object himself.

The poet represents Yussuf as less insensible to her regard than we are informed by Scripture that he really was; and it became necessary that a miracle should be performed, in order to deliver him from the temptations with which he is surrounded, and which are nearly overcoming his resolution. His father, Jacob, or the angel Gabriel in his likeness, appears, to warn him of his danger, and he flies, leaving his

The Rose Garden of Persia

mistress in an agony of despair, rage, and grief. She thus exclaims:—

Is this a dream?—another dream,
Like that which stole my senses first,
Which sparkled o'er my life's dull stream,
By idle, erring fancy nursed?
Was it for this my life I spent
In murmurs deep, and discontent—
Slighted, for this, all homage due,
From gen'rous, faithful love withdrew?
For this, no joy, no pomp have prized;
For this, all honours have despised—
Left all my soul, to passion free,
To be thus hated—spurned—by thee?
O God! to see thee loathing turn,
While on my cheek swift blushes burn;
Contempt, abhorrence on thy brow,
Where radiant sweetness dwelt—till now!
Thy bitter accents, fierce, severe,
In harsh, unwonted tones to hear:
Thy horror, thy disgust to view,
And know thy accusations true!
All, all but this I could have borne,—
A husband's vengeance and his scorn;

Jami

To be reproached, disgraced, reviled,
So Yussuf on his victim smiled.
I would, amidst the desert's gloom,
Have hailed, with thee, a living tomb;
My home, my state, my birth forgot,
And, with thy love, embraced thy lot;
Had taught my heart all pangs to share,
And prove what perfect love can dare.

Let me look back to that dark hour
That bound my spirit to thy power—
Thy grateful words, thy glance recall,
My hopes, my love — and curse them all;
Let me thy tender looks retrace,
The glories of thy heavenly face;
Thy brow, where Aden's splendour lies,
And the mild lustre of thine eyes:
Yet, let my heart no weakness prove,
But hate thee as I once could love.

What fearful eloquence was thine,
What awful anger—just—divine!
Shuddering, I saw my heart displayed,
And knew all this *I* should have said!

The Rose Garden of Persia

'Twas mine to shrink, withstand in time,
For, while I sinned, I knew my crime.

O wretched, wavering heart!—as vain
Thy wild resentment as thy pain:
One thought alone expels the rest,
One sole regret distracts my breast,
O'ermastering and subduing all—
More than my crime, more than my fall:
Are not shame, fear, remorse, forgot,
In that one thought—he loves me not?

The regrets of his unfortunate mistress follow the pure-minded Yussuf to his gloomy prison, where she pictures his sufferings incurred for her crime, and thus laments and strives to derive comfort from reflection:—

Though in a dark and narrow cell
The "fair beloved" confined may dwell,
No prison is that dismal place,
'Tis filled with dignity and grace:
And the damp vaults and gloom around
Are joyous spring, with roses crowned.

Jami

Not Paradise to me were fair
If he were not a dweller there;
Without his presence all is night,
My soul awakes but in his sight:
Though this frail tenement of clay
   May here amidst its pomp remain,
My spirit wanders far away,
   And dwells with his in prisoned pain.

There is now but little variation from the scriptural relations, and Yussuf becomes grand vizir of Egypt, governing with wisdom and skill. Zuleika finds herself a widow: her hopes are renewed, and she is no longer under the necessity of suppressing her affection. She causes a house to be built opposite the residence of the object of her devotion, in order that she may behold him day by day, and hear the sound of his horse's feet as he passes.

Inspired by love, Zuleika at length renounces idolatry, and her lover hails her as a convert to the religion of the only true God. She presents herself as a believer before Yussuf, and is rewarded by the return

The Rose Garden of Persia

of her early youth and beauty, at his prayer;
for he now sees no obstacle to his love, and
at once acknowledges it, and returns the
passion which had been before so fatal to
them both.

YUSSUF'S ACKNOWLEDGMENT

Not love thee!—ah! how much I loved
Long absent years of grief have proved.
Severe rebuke, assumed disdain,
Dwelt in my words and looks in vain:
I would not passion's victim be,
And turned from sin—but not from thee.
My love was pure, no plant of earth
From my rapt being sprung to birth:
I loved as angels might adore,
And sought, and wished, and hoped no
 more.
Virtue was my belov'd: and thou
Hadst virtue's impress on thy brow.
Thy weakness showed how frail is all
That erring mortals goodness call.
I thanked thee, and reproached thee not
For all the sufferings of my lot.

Jami

The God we worship was my friend,
And led me to my destined end,
Taught the great lesson to thy heart
That vice and bliss are wide apart:
And joined us now, that we may prove
With perfect virtue, perfect love.

Nothing now disturbs the tranquillity of their loves, and they live for many years united, until at length Yussuf dies, and his faithful and tender Zuleika, unable to survive his loss, follows him to the tomb. The poem concludes with moral reflections, and an address from the poet to his son.

HATIFI

Abd'allah, surnamed Hatifi, was born at Jâm, in Khorassan. He was nephew to the great poet Jâmi, with whom he lived on more amicable terms than could naturally be expected between rival poets, both so highly distinguished. The ambition of Hatifi was to enter the lists with his uncle, by composing five poems, on the same or similar subjects, with the Khamsah, of that illustrious son of song. Opinions are divided as to whether he succeeded as well as his master, but his sweetness and pathos are unequalled.

However beautiful may be Nizami's exquisite version of the favourite story of Mejnoun and Leila, that of Hatifi is confessedly superior. Hatifi died in A.D. 1520, and was buried in the village of Gardschard.

When he was beginning his great poem,

Hatifi

he begged his uncle to write the first line for him; which he did, and it contained a prophecy of his nephew's future fame. Hatifi's works are *Khosrû and Shireen*; *Heft Manseer*; *Mejnoun and Leila*; and the *Timûr Namah, or Victories of Timûr*.

The subject of the tale of Mejnoun and Leila is extremely simple, and it is said to be founded on fact; it is, in fact, but a repetition of the oft-repeated truth that—

"The course of true love never did run smooth."

Kaïs was the son of an Arabian chief, handsome, amiable, and accomplished beyond all his contemporaries. A fine poet, as the fragments of his verse still repeated with enthusiasm by the Arabs of Hejas prove.

Leila was the daughter of a neighbouring chief. She was equally accomplished with her lover: and nothing seemed likely to disturb the happiness which their permitted attachment promised, till the avarice of her father destroyed at once all their hopes.

The Rose Garden of Persia

Leila was commanded to think of Kaïs no more, as she was destined to be the bride of one more rich and powerful; and, in spite of the grief and remonstrances of the unfortunate pair, they were separated. Kaïs became insane from disappointment, and his name was, therefore, changed to Mejnûn, (the distracted). Death at length put a period to his miseries, and his faithful mistress soon followed him, leaving her cruel parent to his late and vain remorse, and the memory of these victims of avarice to eternal honour and regret.

There are two beautiful expressive couplets by the Moollah of Rûm, characteristic of Eastern brevity and simplicity.

The Khalifah said to Leila, "Art thou the damsel for whom the lost Mejnûn is become a wanderer in the desert? Thou surpassest not other girls in beauty." Leila answered—"Be silent: for thou art not Mejnûn!"

Hatifi

THE MEETING IN THE DESERT

FROM THE POEM OF "MEJNÛN AND LEILA."

Even like the roaming moon, along
   The dreary path fair Leila strayed,
Till, worn and spent the wilds among,
   Deep sleep o'erpowered the lovely maid:
And from her hand the bridle's check
Fell on the patient camel's neck.

The guides were far, and dark the night,
   The weary camel stopped to graze,
The caravan was hid from sight—
   Then lost amidst the desert's maze.
Unconscious still, she wandered on,
And woke—untended and alone!

The Rose was severed from the plain,
   Nor friend nor strangers now intrude:
On through the waste she speeds amain,
   But all is trackless solitude.

The Rose Garden of Persia

From spot to spot, with anxious fear,
She hastes, she calls, but none can hear!
When, from a wild and gloomy height,
A dusky form rushed forth to sight.

No terror seized the maiden's heart—
  A thought sprung there which chilled her dread,
For in that waste, from man apart,
  A life of pain her Kaïs led.
Might not this stranger know his state,
And give her tidings of his fate?

So wasted, worn, and changed with care,
  His mind a void, himself forgot,
The hapless victim of despair—
  Even she, the True One, knew him not!

"Whence com'st thou?" Leila said; "and why
  Amidst these deserts dost thou roam?
Tell me thy name—what destiny
  Has lured thee from thy friends and home?"

Hatifi

The grief-struck youth, unconscious grown,
Knew not his Leila's gentle tone:
"Seek'st thou to know what slave am I,
   For ever doomed a wretch to rove?
'Tis Kaïs, spent with misery—
   'Tis hapless Mejnoon, mad for love!"

The maiden with a sudden bound
Sprang from her camel to the ground:
"Ah! wretched one!—too fondly dear,
A voice, long mute, let Kaïs hear;
Thy saviour let thy Leila be—
Look up—'tis Leila—I am she!"

His mind awoke. One moment's gaze,
One cry of startled, wild amaze!
Though years of madness, grief, and pain,
Had held him in their galling chain,
That magic name has broke the spell,
And prone to earth lost Mejnoon fell.

Scarce less with woe distraught, the maid
   Sat on the ground, his form beside:
His head, which in the dust was laid,
   Upon her knees she drew, and dried

The Rose Garden of Persia

His tears with tender hand, and prest
Him close and closer to her breast:
"Be here thy home, beloved, adored,
Revive, be blest—O Leila's lord!"

At length he breathed—around he gazed,
As from her arms his head he raised.
"Art thou," he faintly said, "a friend
  Who takes me to her gentle breast?
Dost thou, in truth, so fondly bend
  Thine eyes upon a wretch distrest?
Are these thy unveiled cheeks I see—
Can bliss be yet in store for me?

I thought it all a dream, so oft
  Such dreams come in my madness now
Is this thy hand, so fair and soft?
  Is this, in sooth, my Leila's brow?
In sleep these transports I may share,
But when I wake 'tis all despair!

Let me gaze on thee—if it be
An empty shade alone I see;
How shall I bear what once I bore
When thou shalt vanish—as before?"

Hatifi

Then Leila spoke, with smiles all light:
　"To hope, dear wanderer, revive;
Lo! Zemzem's waters cool and bright
　Flow at thy feet—then drink and live.
Seared heart! be glad, for bounteous Heaven
At length our recompense hath given.
Belov'd one! tell me all thy will,
And know thy Leila faithful still.

Here in this desert join our hands,
　Our souls were joined long, long before;
And if our fate such doom demands,
　Together wander evermore.
O Kaïs! never let us part;
　What is the world to thee and me?
My universe is where thou art,
　And is not Leila—all—to thee?"

He clasped her to his aching breast,
　One long, sad, tender look he cast;
Then with deep woe, in vain represt,
　Kissed her fair brow, and spoke at last:—

The Rose Garden of Persia

"How well, how fatally I love,
My madness and my misery prove.
All earthly hopes I could resign—
Nay, life itself, to call thee mine.
But shall I make thy spotless name,
That sacred spell, a word of shame?
Shall selfish Mejnoon's heart be blest,
And Leila prove the Arab's jest?

The city's gates though we may close,
We cannot still the tongues of foes.
No; we have met—a moment's bliss
   Has dawned upon my gloom — in vain!
Life yields no more a joy like this,
   And all to come can be but pain.
Thou, thou—adored!—might be my own,
   A thousand deaths let Mejnoon die
Ere but a breath by slander blown
   Should sully Leila's purity!
Go, then—see where thy tribe return,
   Fly from my arms that clasp thee yet:
I feel my brain with frenzy burn—
   O transport! could I thus forget!"

Hatifi

The frantic lover fled—while near
The tramp of steeds can Leila hear:
Senseless, her mind with anguish torn,
Fair Leila to her tents is borne.
For many a night and many a day
The dark waste saw lost Mejnoon stray:
Bleeding and faint, 'twixt death and life,
Waging with fate unequal strife.
Wild on the blast his words were flung,
Wild to the winds his songs were sung.
The shudd'ring pilgrim, passing by,
Paused as he heard the maniac's cry,
Nor dared upon his lair intrude,
As thus he raved in solitude:—

"How can I live where thou art not?
   In dreams I trace thy image still!
I see thee, and I curse my lot;
   I wake—and all is chill.
The desert's faithless waters spread
   A snare to lure me on:
My thirsty soul is vainly led;
   I stoop—the wave is gone!
The fevered thoughts that on me prey,
Death's sea alone can sweep away.

The Rose Garden of Persia

I found the bird of Paradise,
   That long I sought with care;
Fate snatched it from my longing eyes,
   I held—despair!

Though Khizzer, girt with mystic spell,
   Had seemed to be my guide,
Scarce had I reached the blessed well,
   Its source was dried!

Wail, Leila, wail, our fortunes crost!
Weep, Mejnoon, weep—for ever lost!"

SCHEIK FEIZI

It was said of the great historian Abûl Fazil, that the monarchs of Asia stood more in awe of his pen, than of the sword of Akbar. His brother, Feizi, possessed the gift of poesy in a high degree, and his compositions are highly valued. His Divan consists, like all the greater Divans, or collections of lyric poetry, of two principal divisions, namely, of Kassideh, or the longer elegiac poems, and of Gazelles, sometimes on love, and sometimes on mystic subjects. He mentions himself one which consists of eighteen thousand lines.

The praise of the Shah, Akbar, or *Great*, chiefly engaged his muse; and the monarch certainly merited the name more than any other Indian emperor whose history is recorded. His lighter pieces were such as are called Musk-gazelles, breathing sweetness, and filled with pleasurable ideas, presenting life as a scene of sunshine and summer, where storm and winter are unknown.

In the mystic poems, however, of this author, he approaches nearer to the sublimity of Attar and the great Moollah than any other of their followers; his ideas are tinged with the colour of the Indian belief in which he was brought up. The most remarkable of this collection is called *Serre*, or *Atoms in the Sun*, written in a thousand and one verses (the favourite number in the East): it is partly mystical, and partly philosophical. The title he has chosen is a portion of the mystery which envelops the meaning, and which a Mussulman conceives it proper should always surround divine things. In the part devoted to philosophy, the work treats of the course of the sun through the Zodiac: Brahminical theology is mixed together with the ancient Persian and Indian fire-worship in this singular composition.

The story of Feizi's early life is romantic. He was introduced, when a boy, to the Brahmins, by Sultan Mohammed Akbar,

Scheik Feizi

as an orphan of their tribe, in order that he might learn their language, and obtain possession of their secrets. Feizi became attached to the daughter of the Brahmin who protected him, and she was offered to him in marriage by the unsuspecting father. After a struggle between honour and inclination, the former prevailed, and he confessed to the Brahmin the fraud that had been practised, who, struck with horror, attempted to put an end to his own existence, fearing that he had betrayed his trust, and brought danger and disgrace on his sect.

Feizi, with tears and protestations, entreated him to forbear, promising to submit to any command he might impose on him. The Brahmin consented to live, on condition that Feizi took an oath never to translate the Vedas, nor repeat to any one the creed of the Hindoos.

Feizi, having entered into the desired obligations, parted with his adopted father, bade adieu to his love, and with a sinking heart returned to the sultan. Akbar was greatly mortified to find his scheme had so

The Rose Garden of Persia

signally failed, but he was much touched with the story related to him by the young poet; and, respecting his oath, he forbore to insist on his translating the sacred books, though that was the great object to which he had devoted all his wishes.

The Sultan Akbar was a liberal thinker, and an enlightened searcher after truth, but he gave much offence to his Mohammedan subjects by the favour he showed to the Hindoos.

Feizi composed a work called the *Mahabarit*, which contains the chronicles of the Hindoo princes. From this Ferishta drew largely, in his celebrated history, and amongst the most romantic episodes which he relates is the account of the family of Khaja Aiass. The events occurred about 1606.

Khaja Aiass was a native of Western Tartary, and left his country to try his fortune in Hindostan. He was young and full of hope, but the prospects he had before him were far from encouraging, for he was poor, and his friends were few; he

Scheik Feizi

was accompanied in his expedition by a young wife, who expected soon to become a mother, and was little able to bear the fatigues of their journey. In fact, as they were crossing the desert, hunger, anxiety, and over-exertion overcame her, and she sank exhausted by the way. In this lamentable condition Khaja Aiass found himself the father of a daughter, born under circumstances the most distressing. Their sufferings and adventures in the desert were very great, but at length they reached Lahore, where the Sultan Akbar kept his court. Asiph Khan, one of his principal ministers, was a relation of Aiass, and received him with great kindness; and from one situation of trust to another, he, who had begun his career in so untoward a manner, became in the space of a few years high-treasurer of the empire.

His daughter, born in the desert, was called Mehr-el-Nissar, or the "Sun of Women." As she grew up, she excelled all the ladies of the East in beauty, learning, and accomplishments. She was educated

The Rose Garden of Persia

with the greatest care, and her genius and acquirements soon became the theme of general conversation. She was witty, satirical, ambitious, lofty, and her spirit beyond control. It happened, on one occasion, that Selim, the prince-royal, came to visit her father. When the public entertainment was over, and all but the principal guests were withdrawn, and the wine brought, the ladies, according to custom, were introduced in their veils. Mehr-el-Nissar had resolved to make a conquest of the prince; she therefore exerted all her powers of pleasing, and entirely succeeded in her design. Her dancing and singing enraptured him; and at length, when, as if by accident, she dropped her veil and disclosed her extraordinary beauty, his heart became completely her own. Selim, distracted with love, applied to his father, the sultan, to assist him; but Akbar, aware that the hand of the dangerous beauty was already disposed of, refused to commit an act of tyranny, and in despite of the entreaties and despair of the prince, Mehr-el-

Scheik Feizi

Nissar became the wife of her father's choice, Sheer Afkun, a Turcomanian nobleman of high lineage and great renown.

The bridegroom shortly after, disgusted with the insults and annoyances which he met with from Prince Selim, left the court of Agra, and retired with his wife to Bengal, where he became governor of the province of Burdwan.

When Selim succeeded his father, he recalled Sheer; but he dared not so far outrage public opinion as to deprive the illustrious omrah of his wife. Sheer was a man of exalted feeling, and very popular: his strength and valour rendered him remarkable, and his good qualities endeared him to the people. He had spent his youth in Persia, and had served, with extraordinary renown, Shah Ismael, the chief of the Suvi line. His original name was Asta Fillō, but, having killed a lion, he was dignified with the title of Sheer Afkun, "Destroyer of the Lion," and by that designation became celebrated throughout India. He served in the wars of Akbar with extra-

The Rose Garden of Persia

ordinary reputation, and at the taking of Scinde displayed prodigies of valour.

Selim, now called Jehangire, kept his court at Delhi when Sheer returned. The husband vainly hoped that time had effaced the memory of Mehr-el-Nissar from the monarch's mind; and, being of a noble and trusting disposition, he suspected no treachery. Jehangire had, however, resolved, if possible, to rid himself of his rival.

On one occasion, when they were hunting, he caused him to be exposed to a tiger. Sheer defended himself against the beast in a manner described as perfectly miraculous, without weapons, like a knight of romance, and killed his antagonist. The sultan, unmoved by his valour, next laid a plot to have him trodden to death by an elephant, but he again escaped, having attacked the raging animal and cut off its trunk.

His house was, after this, beset by assassins, and he was in great peril, but once more succeeded in foiling his assailants. His valour and resolution were no match for

Scheik Feizi

the treachery of his powerful foe, and, in the end, the heroic Sheer fell a victim to the persevering cruelty of his rival: he was drawn into an ambush, and fell, after a fearful struggle, pierced with six balls, having killed several of his murderers in the conflict.

Mehr-el-Nissar was now free, and her conduct gave cause of suspicion that her grief was not extreme. She gave out that her husband, being aware of the sultan's attachment to her, had commanded that, in case of his death, she should not long resist his wishes, but surrender herself to him immediately. She was accordingly conveyed, with great care, from Burdwan, where the unfortunate Sheer had, not long before his death, retired, hoping to live with her in peace: and the fair cause of so much mischief was taken to Delhi, to the Sultana-Mother, who received her with every demonstration of respect and affection.

An unforeseen disappointment, however, awaited the beautiful Mehr-el-Nissar: whether actuated by remorse or caprice,

The Rose Garden of Persia

Jehangire, now that no impediment was in the way of his happiness, refused to see her; and she was shut up in one of the worst apartments of his seraglio, where four years were passed by the neglected beauty in such poverty and necessity, that, in order to support herself, she was obliged to employ her talent in various works, which were so exquisite that she obtained a quick sale for them amongst the ladies of Delhi and Agra. By this means she was enabled to repair and beautify her apartments; and she then clothed her attendants in the richest manner, retaining, however, herself, the simplest dress she could devise.

Curiosity, at length, subdued the moody resolve of the sultan; and he determined to see the singular woman, who, under whatever circumstances she appeared, commanded attention. He visited her apartments, where all he saw delighted him—but Mehr-el-Nissar most. He inquired why she made so remarkable a difference between the dress of her slaves and her own; to which question she replied, "Those born to servitude must

Scheik Feizi

dress as it pleases those whom they serve. These are my servants; I alleviate their bondage by every means in my power; but I, that am your slave, O Emperor of the Moghuls! must dress according to your pleasure, not my own."

Charmed with the spirit of this answer, Jehangire at once forgot all his coldness; his former tenderness returned in all its depth, and he resolved to compensate his indifference to the lovely widow by loading her with riches and pomp. The very next day after their tardy interview, a magnificent festival was prepared to celebrate their nuptials. Her name was changed by an edict into Nûr-mâ-hal, the "Light of the Harem." All his former favourites vanished before her, and during the remainder of the reign of Jehangire she bore the chief sway in all the affairs of the empire. She advanced all her family to the highest posts; her numerous relatives poured in from Tartary on hearing of the prosperity of the house of Aiass. Her father, worthy as he was great, sustained his rank with virtue and dignity;

her brothers, also, acquitted themselves, in their several governments, much to the satisfaction of all parties, and no family ever rose so rapidly, or so deservedly, to honour, rank, and eminence as that of Khaja Aiass and his "Desert Born."

THE DESERT BORN

Day fades amidst the mighty solitude,
The sun goes down and leaves no hope behind;
Afar is heard the ravening cry, for food,
Of savage monsters; and the sultry wind
Sears with its furnace-breath, but freshens not,
With one reviving sigh, the dismal spot
Where three devoted beings panting lie,
Prone on the scorching ground,—as if to die
Were all of good could reach their helpless state,
Abandoned, 'midst the trackless sands, to Fate!

Scheik Feizi

And does young Aiass yield to fortune's frown?
Are all his high aspirings come to this?
His haughty bearing to the dust bowed down,
His glorious visions of success and bliss—
The dreams that led him from his Tartar home,
To seek, in golden Hindostan, renown—
Is this the end of all?—Lost, overcome,
By famine and fatigue subdued, at last—
Patience and firmness—hope and valour—past!

He cried—"O Allah! when the Patriarch's child
Forlorn beside his fainting mother lay,
Amidst the howling desert dark and wild,
When not a star arose to cheer her way,
Heard she not Zemzem's murmuring waters nigh,
And the blest angel's voice that said they should not die?

The Rose Garden of Persia

But I—look on my new-born child—look there!
On my young wife—what can I but despair?
She left her tents for me—abandoned all
The wealth, the state her beauty well might claim:
Alas! the guerdon of her truth, how small—
Alas! what had I, but a soldier's name,
A sword—a steed, my faithful, fainting one,
Whose course is, like his master's, almost done?
I led her here to die—to die!—when earth
Has lands so beautiful, and scenes so fair,
Cities and realms, and mines of countless worth;
Monarchs—with proud sultanas all their care,
And none with Zarah worthy to compare!
Yet here she lies—a broken cloud!—this gem,
Fit for the first in India's diadem!

Scheik Feizi

Oh, she was like that tree, all purity,
Which, ere the hand of man approach the bough,
No bird or creeping insect suffers nigh,
Nor shelter to aught evil will allow;
But once the fruit is plucked, there ends the charm—
Dark birds and baneful creatures round it swarm.
Thou, selfish Aiass, hast destroyed the tree;
Behold its lovely blossoms scathed by thee!

Is there no hope?—revive, my noble steed,
Fail not thy master at his utmost need;
Thou canst, thou wilt, support her gentle weight:
Courage!—thou wert not wont to deem it great.
A little further—yet one effort more—
And, if we perish then, our miseries are o'er."

The Rose Garden of Persia

"But oh!—my child!" the fainting
    mother cried,
"My arms are feeble, and support her
    not.
And thou, lost Aiass, death is in thy
    face:
Why should we strive to quit this hideous
    place?
My babe and I can perish by thy side—
Oh! let our graves be in this fatal spot."

She spoke, and prostrate fell. With
    nerveless hands
Her form sad Aiass on his steed has
    cast,
Which, trembling with that lifeless being,
    stands—
His struggling breath comes heavily and
    fast.
A task, a fearful task, must yet be done,
Ere he the Desert's path shall dare ex-
    plore,
His babe must sleep beneath yon tree—
    alone!
No parent's kiss shall ever wake her more.

Scheik Feizi

Some leaves he plucked, the only leaves
 that grew
Upon that mound, so parched and desolate,
These o'er the sleeping innocent he
 threw—
Looked not—nor turned—and left her to
 her fate.

"My babe! thou wert a pearl too
 bright
For pitiless earth's unfriendly slight.
He who first called thee forth again
Shall place thee in thy parent shell:
There shalt thou slumber, free from
 pain,
While guardian Peris watch thee well.
Within our hearts, two living urns,
Shall live thy memory—blessed one!
As the white water-lily turns
Her silver petals to the moon;
Though distance must their loves divide,
And but his image gilds the tide."

The Rose Garden of Persia

THE MOTHER

Oh, who shall tell what horror, what dismay
Flashed wildly from lost Zarah's haggard eye,
When, toiling slowly on their devious way,
Her sense returned, and lo!—her arms no more
She found, with straining clasp, her infant bore!—
She shrieked—O God! that cry of agony
Will Aiass hear for ever. Hark! it rings
Like the death trump, and by its fearful spell
Back all his strength and wasted vigour brings:
He feels unnatural force returning, swell
In all his veins—his blood is flame: that shriek
Resounds again, far through the Desert borne.
What need of words the fatal truth to speak?
What need of questions? is she not forlorn—

Scheik Feizi

Is not a branch torn from the tree
    away,
And will it not—even where it stands—
    decay?

Oh! she had in those few brief hours
Her Desert-born had seen of light,
Gazed in its face, and thought the
    flowers
Of Eden clustered rich and bright
In glory round its radiant brow!—
That all Al Jannat's gems were hid
Beneath that pure and snowy lid.
Where were those heavenly glances
    now?

Oh! as she feebly knelt beside
Its rugged couch, her tears would start,
Lest aught of evil should betide
The cherished idol of her heart.
She traced the father's features there,
In that small tablet, pure and fair,
Exulting in a mother's name:
And in her daughter, nursed the flame
That burned, divided, yet the same.

The Rose Garden of Persia

And has she lost that blessed one!
How lost?—starved—left to beasts a prey!
Was deed so fell by Aiass done—
Her own beloved, her hope, her stay?
Has misery changed her heart to stone?
"My child! my child!" she shrieks: the Desert wild
Returned in hollow yells—"Give back my child!"

THE BLACK SNAKE

With flashing eye and rapid pace,
Of hope, of fear, alike bereft,
Flies Aiass, guided by the trace
His courser's tottering steps had left
Along the deep and sandy way,
Back where his poor deserted infant lay.

Beneath a tree, the single one
That in the Desert sprang alone—
Like latent hope, that, struggling, will
Live in the tortured bosom still—

Scheik Feizi

Slumbering and peaceful lay the child;
A faint and tender roseate streak
Had dawned along its hollow cheek,
And in unconscious dreaming bliss—it smiled.

But—coiled around it—peering in
To the closed eyes and tranquil face,
Winding its dark rings on the ivory skin,
A black snake holds it in his fell embrace;
His forked tongue and fiery eyes reveal,
The helpless infant's fate one moment more shall seal!
With frantic shout the father onward sprung,
While yet the serpent to his victim clung;
The monster, startled from his prey,
Quelled by a human glance, relaxed his hold,
With sudden bound unloosed each slimy fold,
And 'midst the rocky billows slunk away.
One frenzied spring—and to his panting breast
Aiass his wakened, rescued treasure prest.

The Rose Garden of Persia

With step, than antelope's less fleet,
The happy father fled away,
And where his weeping Zarah lay,
Cast his loved burden at her feet.
His brain reels round, his short-lived vigour flies;
Prostrate he falls, and darkness veils his eyes.

THE CARAVAN

Oh, wild is the waste where the caravan roves,
And many the danger the traveller proves;
But the star of the morning shall beckon him on,
And blissful the guerdon his patience has won;
Nor water, nor milk, nor fresh dates shall he need,
No loss has he met of good camel or steed,

Scheik Feizi

He looks o'er the sands as a road to renown,
For the hills in the distance his labour shall crown:
He sings of Shiraz, and her generous wine,
And pours to the prophet libations divine;
The numbers of Hafiz awake in his song,
And who shall declare that the poet is wrong?

GAZEL

To-day is given to pleasure,
   It is the feast of spring;
And earth has not a treasure
   Our fortune shall not bring.

Fair moon! the bride of heaven confest,
   Whose light has dimmed each star,
Show not thy bright face in the East,
   My love's outshines it far.

The Rose Garden of Persia

Why sighs the lonely nightingale,
  Ere day's first beams appear?
She murmurs forth her plaintive tale
  For coming Spring to hear.

O ye severely wise,
  To-day your counsels spare;
Your frown in vain denies
  The wine-cup and the fair.

Within our haunts of bliss
  The dervish may be seen,
Whose seat, till days like this,
  Within the mosque has been.

I care not—but the truth declare,
  That Hafiz fills again:
His eyes are on his charming fair,
  His lips the wine-cup drain.

'Twas near a fountain's brink a group reclined,
Where waters sported with the morning wind,

Scheik Feizi

Trees threw their shadows broad and deep
    around,
And grass, like emeralds, freshened all the
    ground.
All former care and future toil forgot,
They hailed the present in this happy
    spot:
Merchants they were, and great their
    treasured store,
Rich musk from Khoten, gems and stuffs
    they bore,
Bound o'er the desert sands to fair Lahore.
From climes remote, and different nations,
    some
Amidst these arid tracts were bent to roam
In search of pleasure, wandering from
    their home.
They sang their country's legends as they
    lay,
And soothed with melody the devious
    way:
One dark-eyed minstrel lured the curious
    throng,
To list the Brahmin's sad, mysterious
    song.

The Rose Garden of Persia

LAY OF BRIMHA'S SORROW

Minstrel, wake the Magic spell!
Sing of Love, its wonders tell;
  Tell how it subdues the proud.
Shall we blame weak man that falls,
When thy glowing verse recalls
  How immortal natures bowed,
How great Brimha's heart was tried,
How for woman's love he sighed?

Who shall say where love begins,
How its subtle way it wins?
Gods, who love the race they frame,
Cannot tell whence springs the flame.
Man may reason long and well,
But can never break the spell.

Sing of Brimha, and the pain
Which disturbs his sacred reign;
Even on his heavenly throne
  Tears of sorrow cloud his eye,
Dreaming of that fatal one,
  Born in awful mystery:

Scheik Feizi

Last created—prized the most,
Beauteous, loving, loved, and lost!

Sometimes when the stars look dim,
   And the moaning winds are high,
Brimha wakes his mournful hymn,
   Tuned to grief that cannot die.

THE GOD'S LAMENT

Then farewell!—since 'tis a crime,
   Being, beautiful as day,
To adore thee through all time,
Since I may not call thee mine,
Nor before thy glance divine,
   Gaze my own rapt soul away.

Ill my anxious toil repaid me,
Fatal was the power that made thee
   Others may behold those eyes,
Others live for ages blest,
   I must seek my native skies,
Robbed of hope, of peace, and rest.

The Rose Garden of Persia

Thou wilt make the world all light,
But my throne is endless night.

From my heart thy being came,
Springing from its purest flame.
   Little deemed I that the last,
Brightest of my works would be—
   As my eager glances fast
   On the perfect form I cast—
Fatal to my power and me!

Of the lotus flower I chose
   Leaves the freshest for thine eyes,
Flowers whose petals never close,
   And whose colours are the sky's:
For thy hair, the clouds that fleet
   O'er the radiant face of heaven;
And the waves thy dancing feet
   All their rapid play had given;
Every bud of purest race,
Was combined to form thy face;
All the powers my prescience knew,
In one mighty work I threw;
All its force my mind employed—
And the close its peace destroyed!

Scheik Feizi

Fain would I the task forget
   Which has charmed each sense so long,
For its guerdon is regret,
   And its memory breathes of wrong.
Not one hope can Fate allow:
'Tis a crime to love thee now!

Vainly is the world created,
   Vainly may it rise or fall;
Dead to joy, with triumph sated,
   'Tis to me a desert all.
All is nothing without thee,
Yet thy name is death to me!

Death?—ah, would that death could come,
   And my long despair be o'er!
But in my eternal home,
   I must mourn for evermore.
Weeping, even as Rudder wept,
Tears that in oblivion slept,
Till the din of mortal strife
Called his being into life.
Floods of tears he gave to me,
And the saddest flow for thee.

The Rose Garden of Persia

Farewell, child of beauty!—go
Bless and gladden all below;
Turn thine eyes to heaven in prayer,
And behold a lover there,
Who renounced, for thy dear sake,
 All the bliss of earth combined:
Save the joys his power might take,
 And to virtue all resigned.

. . . .

A shriek!—what sound is through the stillness sent?—
All pause, all listen, breathless and intent,
Even the sagacious camels cease to graze,
The coursers sniff the air with eager gaze:
And anxious voices soon their counsel lent—
"Some traveller, lost amidst the desert's maze,
Demands our care,—on—on ere yet too late,
Snatch we our brother from impending fate."
And thus was Aiass saved. And at that hour
Arose the star that shed its guiding power,

Scheik Feizi

To lead him on to wealth, and pomp, and state;
The noblest, highest 'midst the proud and great.

And bards have told the fortunes of that child,
Exposed to famine in the dreary wild,
Whose peerless beauty and whose mighty fame
Have filled the world with Mehr-el-Nissar's name!

www.ingramcontent.com/pod-product-compliance
Lightning Source LLC
Chambersburg PA
CBHW011341090426
42743CB00018B/3399